Truth, lies **and** Science education

Paul Taylor

© Day One Publications 2007
First printed 2007

ISBN 978-1-84625-071-2

9 781846 250712 >

ISBN 978-1-84625-071-2

British Library Cataloguing in Publication Data available

Published by Day One Publications
Ryelands Road, Leominster, HR6 8NZ
☎ 01568 613 740 FAX 01568 611 473
email—sales@dayone.co.uk
web site—www.dayone.co.uk
North American—e-mail—sales@dayonebookstore.com
North American—web site—www.dayonebookstore.com

Designed by Steve Devane and printed by Gutenberg Press, Malta

Contents

Appreciations

Paul Taylor, in this book, argues cogently for it being essential to keep a moral dimension to our teaching of secondary school science. Here he develops a thesis that to divorce the two ultimately is to lose the definition of knowledge itself. In our postmodern culture we have tried to separate 'values' from the 'facts'. We have wrongly set up a duality such that the spiritual is not mandatory and can be reckoned to be a matter of opinion, and just facts on their own (all the physical world around us) can be studied without any reference to values, and certainly no absolutes from non-material thinking. How wrong we are is the thrust of this book based on the Master's thesis of Paul Taylor with the University of Wales (Cardiff) in 2000. Paul is a keen thinker and has thought widely not only on the issues of creation versus evolution, but of the far wider social deconstruction which has removed the whole basis of the Western sense of truth and even rationality. Only the Christian gospel founded in Genesis can rebuild the next generation.

Professor Andy McIntosh. DSc, FIMA, C.Math, FEI, C.Eng, FInstP, MIGEM, FRAeS, University of Leeds

Sending a child to a state school may be the only option, but the child will often be exposed to an atheistic worldview which can have a damaging effect on his or her spiritual development. Christian parents who send their children to state schools must understand how atheistic values have crept into many areas of the school curriculum. This book by Paul Taylor will greatly help parents identify and deal with the problems that their children face in state schools.

Stuart Burgess, BSc (Eng), PhD, CEng, FIMechE, FRAeS, Professor of Design & Nature, Head of Department of Mechanical Engineering, University of Bristol

Students spend more time with their teachers/professors than they do with their parents in learning to understand what life is all about. As a result, their formalized education has a great impact on their worldview. Truth, Lies and Science Education *is a valiant attempt to tackle this issue head on to engage the education system and parents in understanding the realities of what is being taught to children and how they are being conformed to a secular way of thinking about every aspect of reality.*

Ken Ham, President of Answers in Genesis, USA

Foreword

It gives me great pleasure to write the Foreword to what I believe is one of the most important books ever written about the teaching of science in the classrooms of schools in the UK. Most of us are totally unaware of what actually goes on in the teaching environment in the classroom. Yes, I know we attend parents' evenings and discuss with teachers the progress, or otherwise, of our children in the classroom. I know how we help with (and sometimes actually *do*) our children's homework. Parents and grandparents will talk with their children and grandchildren, respectively, about what they are taught, but the children are unable to explain *why* they are taught what they are taught or what the philosophical ideologies behind the teaching are.

Christians, as well as non-Christians, ought to be aware of the *spiritual* dimension of what is taught in the classroom. Most people think, wrongfully as it turns out, that teaching is 'neutral' in the sense that it has no spiritual dimension—that it is totally unrelated to whether there is a God or not, and that it matters not whether the teacher believes in God or not. Paul Taylor concludes otherwise.

The author is well qualified to explore the spiritual nature of the science that is taught in the UK National Curriculum. Firstly, Paul Taylor has taught science in secondary schools and was head of science for a number of years at a large comprehensive school in South Wales. Secondly, he has been awarded an MEd by the University of Wales for his dissertation entitled *Science and Spirituality in the National Curriculum*. It is a real eye-opener to realize that the science teaching is not neutral and that what is taught in the classroom reflects the spiritual belief system (whether atheistic, agnostic, Christian or otherwise) of those who compiled the science syllabus of the National Curriculum, as well as those who teach it. This will be an unsettling conclusion to Christian parents because it means that much of the God-centred teaching that their children receive at home and church is negated by the teaching received in school, as the science taught in the National Curriculum is not God-centred and certainly most of the science teachers in our schools are not Christians.

Paul Taylor exposes many errors that are taught as truth in the science lessons that are laid down by the National Curriculum—in biology, the earth sciences, chemistry and physics. Without wishing to steal the author's thunder, I could mention that perhaps one of the most serious errors that thousands of students have been taught, and still are being taught, is that natural selection is demonstrated conclusively by the peppered moth. Yet in the late 1990s the results of the experiments performed on peppered moths some forty years earlier, and which allegedly showed that they are subject to natural selection, are fraudulent. One can only wonder why this is still being taught in our classrooms. The only conclusion that can be drawn is that it is taught to strengthen a belief in godless, atheistic evolution.

The findings and conclusions of this book are disturbing. Every parent should be aware that the teaching of science is not neutral, but it is biased—biased toward the teaching that there is no God; that there is no creator; that there are no (God-given) rules by which we have to live our lives; and that there is no God to whom we have to give an account. In this book, Paul Taylor ensures that every parent knows that his or her children are being taught science in a manner that has its roots more in the faith system of the educators than they would care to acknowledge.

I can warmly commend this book to everyone that has an interest in the education of our young people.

Dr A J Monty White
Chief Executive
Answers in Genesis (UK/Europe)

Since August 2005, I have been employed as a writer and speaker and Head of Media and Publications at Answers in Genesis (UK/Europe). Answers in Genesis is an evangelistic ministry, seeking to uphold the truth of the Bible from the very first verse. As such, it stands against secular, non-biblical worldviews such as NeoDarwinian evolution and millions of years.

I compiled my dissertation for my Master of Education degree (Cardiff University of Wales: 2000) on the topic 'Science and Spirituality in the National Curriculum'.

The title was inspired by an interesting phrase in the document 'Science in the National Curriculum'. This National Curriculum document, frequently revised, has prescribed what should be taught in schools in England, Wales and Northern Ireland in the name of science, since the early 1990s (Scotland has its own curriculum). Since devolution in 1999, there have been slight differences in the documents of these three constituent areas of the UK, such as the requirement in Wales to include the *Curriculum Cymreig*—teaching elements of the syllabus, using examples from a specifically Welsh context, where possible. However, none of these differences from the document in force in England are sufficiently significant, in areas pertaining to science, to merit a separate treatment. Moreover, many of the attitudes taken to the teaching of science are likely to find their echo elsewhere, so these studies will have implications for education in Scotland, and in other countries.

Some people have suggested that I prepare a version of the dissertation for publication. I have attempted to do this in this book. However, I have had three reservations to overcome.

1. My dissertation was necessarily an academic work, written in a formal academic style. I prefer my arguments to be more accessible. Therefore, I have changed the style of language in the present work, forfeiting the formal, passive voice, impersonal style, and adopting a more personal, active-voice style. More academically minded people might regret this, and feel that the arguments are thereby diminished. However, I felt that I wanted to get my views across to a wider audience, who might be put off by an academically styled work.

2. In order for my dissertation to be acceptable for a secular university

readership, my arguments in the dissertation are of a more general nature than I would have liked. My actual views on education are rooted in my understanding of the Bible and how it applies to the world today. Therefore, the present work is an attempt to restore this important biblical context.

3. In the years since I wrote my Master's dissertation, my views have developed and changed somewhat. Although my overall philosophy and commitment to the truth of the Bible remain the same, I have added new material to this book to reflect these changes. Some of this quotes literature which was unavailable at the time of writing my original dissertation. One area where my views have developed is this: at the time of writing the dissertation, I was firmly wedded to the idea of state-run comprehensive education. I am now an advocate of independent Christian schools and home education. Finally, I have added a considerable amount of new material since joining the staff of Answers in Genesis, about how science education is to be viewed, in the light of a biblical approach to the subject.

Though the present work is clearly directed towards the education scenes in England and Wales, which I know best, I hope that the lessons drawn will be applicable in many other situations, where Christians rub shoulders with the education world. If readers from other countries have extra examples that I could add to sections on the outworking of science syllabuses in the classroom, then I will be glad to receive them, and will do my utmost to incorporate them into future editions of the book.

A number of people deserve a special mention, as they have contributed to this work.

Special thanks go to Anthony Packer, retired lecturer and tutor from Cardiff University. Anthony supervised my Master's dissertation, which forms the basis of the present work. The dissertation was written at a time of great personal stress for me, and during our meetings, he became as much a friend as tutor. It was also Anthony who first urged that I revisit the material and prepare it for publication for a wider audience.

I am deeply grateful to Dr Monty White for his support for this work. His current role as my boss (CEO of *Answers in Genesis* [UK/Europe]) and his previous as Administrator at Cardiff University meant that he understood the need for a work on education such as this. I am indebted to him for his agreeing to write the Foreword to this book.

I am also grateful to the following people, who agreed to provide their comments on the book for the cover. I value their advice: Ken Ham, founder of *Answers in Genesis*, and President of AiG-USA, Professor Andy McIntosh of Leeds University, Professor Stuart Burgess of Bristol University, and Steve Layfield, Head of Science at Emmanuel College, Gateshead.

Thanks are also due to the editorial team at DayOne Publications for helpful suggestions.

Most of all, I want to thank my children, Gemma, Adam and Jack. We have been through such a lot of crises together, but your respective faiths have not wavered. You have all three endured some of the negatives of state education described in these pages, but the commitment of all of you to truth has seen you through

The spiritual context of the science curriculum

Behind the curriculum

Many editions of the National Curriculum have contained the enigmatic phrase 'Pupils should be taught ... the social, moral, historical and spiritual contexts of science'.[1] All of these aspects of science have proved controversial, in their own time. For example, a study of the use of coal as a fuel may lead to a discussion of the history of the coal industry in the South Wales valleys. Indeed, this context might be deemed compulsory in the Welsh National Curriculum, where there is a constant requirement to teach within the *Curriculum Cymraeg* (Welsh Curriculum). But how confident does the average chemistry teacher feel about the issue?

In the 1980s, some schools advocated the teaching of 'peace studies' across the curriculum. There was pressure to include this in the teaching about nuclear energy. Can the teaching about using the nucleus of fissile atoms as a source of energy ever be divorced from a discussion of the merits or demerits of nuclear energy? How confident would the average physics teacher feel about leading a classroom debate on the subject?

Does the subject of human reproduction merit a discussion, among teenage pupils, of the rights and wrongs of premarital sex? How could such a lesson proceed, given that many of the biology teachers concerned might themselves be living with a partner, unmarried? Should the lesson, which discusses the development of human embryos and foetuses, also include a debate on the moral justification, or otherwise, of abortion?

It is possible that such issues might cause a degree of increasing discomfort for many classroom teachers. While some teachers may be comfortable with encouraging pupils to consider the moral implications of scientific studies, it is not clear that much study has been done on the teaching of the spiritual implications of science.

Chapter 1

It can be argued that all schools teach a hidden curriculum. The first school, at which I taught, specifically admitted this. In the staff handbook of the school, the hidden curriculum was taken to mean the values imparted to the pupils by the ethos of the school and the behaviour of the staff, without being formally taught. It was assumed that the teacher in the classroom was imparting values to his or her pupils. This belief is hard to find among teachers today, who would argue that they are, and should be, morally neutral. Robin Barrow is Professor of the Philosophy of Education at the University of London. He says this:

We cannot contemplate life without morality, and therefore we cannot take seriously the suggestion that moral education is not important or might be set aside.[2]

Barrow makes this comment in spite of the fact that he argues against the teaching of religion. Nevertheless, he sees the need for moral education. Another educational philosopher, P. H. Hirst, suggests the sort of values that might be taught in such a way. Hirst is Professor of Education at the University of London's Institute of Education.

There is 'discrimination among values'. This includes the distinction of various kinds of value and their relative importance, an awareness of the values of character like fair play and self-control, intellectual values like the love of truth and aesthetic values like good taste, and, in addition, a commitment to such values in the conduct of life.[3]

The above quote begs a number of questions to which we will need to return later. For example, who determines relative importance of values and against which yardstick? How does the teacher instil into the pupil a love of truth, if the teacher knows or suspects that some of what she is teaching to her class is incorrect? Nevertheless, Christian educationalists have agreed with the above approach, on the basis that the most important values to them will be those guided by what they find in the Bible. Roques believes that teachers need to enable children to have a sense of awe of creation, and, by implication, the Creator:

Children and young people need to see that this world we inhabit is the stunning playground of our Father in heaven. We must not allow our children to lose this sense of mystery as they gaze at Ron the porcupine or Ralph the badger.[4]

Roques, who is a tutor for the 'Thinking Space Gap Year Programme' of the West Yorkshire School of Christian Studies, is suggesting that this 'sense of mystery' is an important teaching point, but that it is not taught explicitly. It must, therefore, form part of the 'hidden curriculum' of a science teacher. When science is being taught, it is not just the subject matter of the lesson at hand that is being taught. The student also learns something practical about the nature of science. In a lesson where a student is planning an experimental investigation, the student also learns the importance of scientific enquiry; the formulation of testable hypotheses, and the testing of these by observational experiment. Conversely, when a student is told that Darwin's theory of evolution is the correct explanation of life, and any explanation requiring God is non-scientific, he or she develops the understanding that some areas of science are sacrosanct and not to be questioned. Roques underlines this point when he says:

A given paradigm is intimately connected to 'ontological' commitments. Philosophical theories of reality (materialism, idealism, Cartesian dualism, Aristotelian hylomorphism etc) betray our worldview commitments. Such theories articulate at a theoretical level how we understand or slice up reality. These ontological theories are accordingly rooted in our ultimate or religious commitments. So, if a person or community believes that matter is self-existent, then this religious belief will control what a person takes to be 'the facts'.[5]

The history of national curriculum science

Since the inception of the National Curriculum in English and Welsh education in the late 1980s, the 'Nature of Science' has formed an integral part of the science programme of study. The National Curriculum in science has taken many forms, and the relevant section has had a variety of names—currently appearing under the section entitled 'Scientific Enquiry'. The original consultative document contained twenty two Attainment Targets, grouped into four Profile Components. When the curriculum itself was promulgated later in the same year, it contained seventeen Attainment Targets in two profile components. This was later deemed to be too complicated, so Profile Components were abandoned and the whole edifice was merged into four Attainment Targets in the second edition of 1991, which were retained in the third edition, published in 1995. It is noteworthy, however, in the context of the original work, that the second edition contained the following fascinating senyence:

Pupils should be given opportunities to develop their knowledge and understanding of how scientific ideas change through time and how their nature and the use to which they are put are affected *by the social, moral, spiritual and cultural contexts* in which they developed.[6]

Many publications, both before and since that declaration, have concentrated on the social and cultural contexts of science and many science teachers have sought to address moral issues. However, the question of what exactly is meant by the spiritual context of science, and how it can be taught, is of considerable significance, and is the central concern of this work.

While the phrasing of the second edition provides the starting point for the current work, it must be pointed out that the 1995 version of 'Science in the National Curriculum' replaces the phrase italicised above with the expression 'affected by the social and historical contexts'. However, in 1997, the Department for Education and Skills considered that the word 'historical' included cultural, spiritual and moral, and did not consider that the 1995 version had changed the emphasis of the 1991 version.[7] With devolution in 1999, Wales got its own National Curriculum based on the 1995 version, where the word 'spiritual' did not specifically appear. England got a new version of 'Science in the National Curriculum' in 2000, in which the word 'spiritual' had reappeared.

The frequent revision of the National Curriculum, which has taken place since its first publication, has affected teachers' attitudes towards it. Notably, the updating of schemes of work implied by the curriculum has needed to be accompanied by updating of bought resources. This means that many teachers have probably given little time to the broader study of concepts of science, particularly within the spiritual context. For pragmatic reasons, teachers are more likely to have opened their National Curriculum documents at the pages referring to their subjects, i.e. to Life Processes, Material Processes and Physical Processes, which are largely euphemisms for the traditional areas of biology, chemistry and physics. These are Attainment Targets 2, 3 and 4 respectively. Many teachers would maintain that the substance of the science syllabus is what matters, and little time is spent on its context, with little or no time on the issue of science and spirituality. However, what soon becomes clear is that spiritual values pervade all science teaching. Scientific facts and theories are always taught within the contexts of the teachers' own worldview or the prevailing worldview of the contexting society.

Roques' work emphasises this point:

Our modern secular culture has convinced most of us that 'science' has nothing to do with 'religion'. It is completely neutral, objective and unshaped by religious prejudice … Science, be it chemistry, physics or biology, is always practised in the light of a person's worldview.[8]

He goes on to quote from a textbook called *Scientific Eye*, written by broadcaster and writer, Adam Hart-Davies:

Two hundred years ago no one could have guessed that the black moths might take over Birmingham. No one can now guess what will make *you* the fittest for the life ahead. Look around the class. All the children are different. Some have curly hair. Some have blue eyes. Some have brown skin. Some can run fast. Some can scream loudly. At school, the best things to be good at are probably exams, whispering and not annoying teachers. The colour of your hair, your eyes and your skin doesn't matter much.[9]

Roques comments that to demonstrate such an attitude betrays a spiritual view on the part of the author. 'This passage is most revealing in that the theme of fitness is extended into the lives of children. Good behaviour is preferable because it will increase one's ability to survive.'[10] His argument proposes that the child who has understood this view of the world will presumably believe it to be factual rather than hypothetical, and will draw conclusions beyond the behavioural conclusion drawn by Hart-Davies. Roques asks about the view of happiness encouraged by the quotation and asks whether it implies that we will be 'happy if we love our enemies', suggesting probably not, as it would seem more advisable to get rid of them.[11] He is concerned about the spirituality presented to pupils by such literature, observing: 'It is all the more disturbing that this worldview is simply presented as "fact". And we all know that you can't argue with the facts '[12]

Roques's contention is that it is disingenuous to claim that a 'neutral' science be taught (i.e. science without values) by the National Curriculum. He asserts that the science that teachers present to pupils 'carries a message with it'. The implicit message is always a message of values, in his terms, which intrinsically reflect spiritual values. The message carried is, however, the suggestion that 'scientists should have no spiritual values', a statement which would seem to be, by paradoxical implication, a declaration of spiritual values by negation. (It is perhaps by the same reasoning that Yellow-Pages directories sometimes list the humanist societies under the category of 'Religious Organisations') It is, of course, a matter of concern that it should do so as the jargon of the National Curriculum has become so much a part of the teacher's life and vocabulary that its rooted philosophies are scarcely discussed any more. Teachers themselves are now so acculturated with its assumptions that it can come as a shock to realise that the vocabulary of the National Curriculum is still something of a foreign language to many from outside the education world. Wragg and Partington described the alienation felt by a recently appointed parent governor, struggling to make sense of it all. The late Ted Wragg was known for his TV and radio comments on education. He was Professor of Education at Exeter University. John Partington—a former tutor of this author—lectured in education at Nottingham University.

'I sit through meetings ... knowing little or nothing about several of the things we discuss.' Governors are usually reluctant to stop meetings so that someone can explain the GCSE, profiling, the changing role of the LEA,[13] or whatever.[14]

Such a response can be explained by the bewilderingly fast pace of change that the National Curriculum has brought about in a relatively short time.

When the author began teaching, in 1983, there was no National Curriculum. At that time, each school produced its own curriculum, although it is fair to comment that a common interest was focused by the need to present students for public examinations. Since that time, the principle of local autonomy has been replaced by the National Curriculum. In science, this has seen four editions in fifteen years, not to mention the consultative documents produced between editions. There has been a concerted attempt, not only to impose its prescriptions on schools and their pupils, but to develop a uniform pattern of understanding, which all teachers are required to share. It is a context that makes it imperative that fundamental principles of machinery, which involve all of us, are regularly scrutinised, in order that no false assumption goes unexamined. The consequences of failing to do so will lead to the encouragement of a consistent lack of freedom of thought.

Spirituality in national curriculum science

In order to discern how these matters influence our theme of spirituality in science education, it is worth considering the evolution of thought behind National Curriculum science. 'Science 5 to 16' was a document published by the DES[15] in 1987. It was a major turning point. Schools and LEAs were urged to see science teaching as an integrated continuum throughout a child's education, from the age of five to the age of sixteen. This concept, seemingly so obvious today, was an innovation at the time, as it decreed that science education was to start from an understanding of the child's experiences at the age of five. Each successive year's teaching would build on a previously established foundation. This concept was novel indeed and contrasted with the traditional concept of science education, in which universities determined the content of A-levels,[16] which in turn determined the content of O-levels[17] and CSEs.[18] Teachers were still digesting the implications of this perspective, when the consultative document was superseded by the National Curriculum for science, which divided science teaching, in an unprecedented fashion, into four Profile Components.

This regrouping of the curriculum structure was of the greatest importance, as a Profile Component was to be a category for the assessment of pupils' abilities, while the newly introduced concept of

Chapter 1

Attainment Targets categorised science under different headings. The implied 'Levels of Attainment' were to indicate the pupil's ability, by criterion referencing, on a scale of 1 to 10. The Programme of Study, which was delivered through these structures, was the statutory body of syllabus content. However, the Profile Components cut across the traditional scientific divides of biology, chemistry and physics in a revolutionary way. These Profile Components were based on a didactic classification rather than traditional disciplines. That is to say, they were based on different aspects of science teaching methodology. Thus they included components on investigation, recording and the nature of science, as well as criterion-related reference to knowledge and understanding. This complicated formula was then simplified a little, leaving 17 Attainment Targets in the first definitive edition of 'Science in the National Curriculum (1989)'. Attainment Target 17 was called 'The Nature of Science' and required teachers to show their pupils that scientific ideas are not immutable laws, but are subject to development. This Attainment Target was imposed with the intention of ensuring that pupils would tackle questions of controversy and debate within the scientific community, and the Programme of Study for this Attainment Target stated:

Pupils ... should ... consider how the development of a particular scientific idea or theory relates to its historical, and cultural—including the spiritual and moral—context.[19]

The Statements of Attainment, which relate to this target, stated, for example, at level 4 that pupils should:

Be able to give an account of some scientific advance, for example, *in the context of medicine, agriculture, industry or engineering*, describing the new ideas and investigation or invention and the life and times of the principle [*sic*] scientist involved.[20]

At higher levels, it was suggested that there might be discussion along the lines being investigated by the present work. Level 7 stated that pupils should:

Be able to give an historical account of a change in accepted theory or explanation and demonstrate an understanding of its effects on people's lives—physically, socially, spiritually and morally, for example … *Galileo's dispute with the Church*.[21]

As already noted, the development of National Curriculum science was a complex and often confusing process. Shortly before the first assessments at Key Stage 3 were to take place in 1991, the then DES published the second edition of the National Curriculum, which removed the Profile Components of the science curriculum. Science was now divided into four Attainment Targets (ATs), of equal weighting, called Scientific Investigation, Life and Living Processes, Materials and their Properties and Physical Properties. It was recognised by science teachers that ATs 2, 3 and 4 were euphemisms for biology, chemistry and physics. The realisation was a logistical nightmare for some schools, which had already dismantled these three traditional subdivisions, and had reorganised their science departments into inter-discipline areas, using the new ATs. Some felt that they had reorganised into a *cul-de-sac*. Moreover, each AT was now split into strands, to reflect the traditional divisions of the sciences. Physical Processes was now divided into 'Electricity and Magnetism', 'Energy Resources and Energy Transfer', 'Forces and their Effects', 'Light and Sound' and 'The Earth's Place in the Universe'. The innovative ideas of the former AT 17, seen by many as esoteric, seemed to have been displaced. However, when teachers read the introduction to the Programme of Study, they were to discover that there would be a requirement to teach
a. Communication
b. The application and economic, social and technological implications of science
c. The nature of scientific ideas.
It was apparent that this third strand replicated the former AT 17, as it was now required that:

Pupils should be given opportunities to develop their knowledge and understanding of how scientific ideas change through time and how their nature and the use to which they are put are affected by the social, moral, spiritual and cultural contexts in which they are developed.[22]

We can see from this examination of the process by which the new science curriculum was decided, that the word 'spiritual' was clearly present in both the 1989 and 1991 versions of the National Curriculum. If we trace the documentation, we notice that the 1989 version seemed to propose that 'spiritual' was a sub-set of 'historical'. However, the 1995 version (published by the renamed Department for Education [DfE], which invited satirists to suggest that there was a Department *against* education— probably the Treasury) retained the same four Attainment Targets as the 1991 version. It also contained a preamble to the Programme of Study, in which a section entitled 'The Nature of Scientific Ideas' stated that:

Pupils should be given opportunities to … consider ways, in which scientific ideas may be affected by the social and historical contexts in which they develop.[23]

This was in a context, which made it plain that the DfE considered that the 'historical' context also includes cultural, moral and spiritual aspects.

The word 'spiritual' was reinstated in the 2000 edition of the National Curriculum in England, though not, strangely, in Wales.

Practical teaching of science in a spiritual context

The discussion above has shown that, during the development of the National Curriculum, teachers underwent a process, which many found to be confusing. There was, therefore, a clear temptation to reduce the impact of innovative ideas to a minimum. Since the National Curriculum intended pupils to be assessed on the basis of their achievements, matched against the criteria laid down in the Levels of Attainment, there was a reluctance to donate valuable teaching time to aspects which were not to be directly examined. Such non-examined comments included those to be found as statements of policy, within the preamble to the Programme of Study, including, as we have seen above, reference to the teaching of science within a spiritual context. In the next chapter, however, it will be argued that the teaching of science has an inevitable spiritual context, even if the teacher is unaware at the point of delivery of the curriculum. It will be argued that it would be better for this hidden spiritual context to be examined so that a more balanced approach to this context of science may be achieved. Furthermore, it should be noted that the frame of reference deployed in the present discussion is one which relates primarily to a Christian understanding of this term. This is despite the fact that the National Curriculum is often framed in terms of a multi-ethnic and multi-cultural view of religious education, and also does not commit itself to any equivalence between the concept of the spiritual and the idea of committed religious practice

For the Christian, it is important to analyse the methodology and pedagogy of science teaching from a biblical perspective. If, as this work attempts to justify, current science teaching in state schools is not neutral, but actually presents a secular philosophy to students, then it is incumbent on Christians to take an informed position on this issue. This will have profound implications on the delivery of science curricula in various spheres—notably, a Christian teacher in a secular state school, a teacher in a Christian school and the educational awareness of a Christian parent.

Notes

1   See, for example, *Science in the National Curriculum*, (London: H.M.S.O., 1989), p. 36.

2   **R. Barrow,** *The Philosophy of Schooling* (Brighton: Wheatsheaf, 1981), p. 177.

3   **P.H. Hirst,** *Knowledge and the Curriculum* (London: Routledge, 1974), p. 34.

4   **M. Roques,** *Curriculum Unmasked, Towards a Christian Understanding of Education* (Eastbourne: Monarch, 1989), p. 20.

5   Ibid. p. 83.

6   *Science in the National Curriculum* (London: Cassell Education, 1991), p. 21.

7   Correspondence from **David Blunkett,** Secretary of State for the Department for Education and Skills (1997) to a former teacher colleague of the author.

8   **Roques,** *Curriculum Unmasked,* p. 153.

9   **A. Hart-Davies,** *Scientific Eye* (London: Bell and Hyman, 1985), p. 54.

10 **Roques,** *Curriculum Unmasked,* p. 5

11 Ibid. p. 75.

12 Ibid. p. 81.

13 LEA stands for Local Education Authority: those departments of local councils in the UK, which oversee schools and education.

14 E.C. Wragg and **J.A. Partington,** *The School Governors' Handbook* (2nd edn, London: Routledge, 1989), p. 96.

15 The Education Department changes its name more frequently that its socks. This abbreviation stood for Department of Education and Science.

16 School matriculation exams, usually taken by pupils at the age of 18.

17 School matriculation exams for the age of 16, traditionally marking the end of compulsory education. O-levels and CSEs were replaced in 1987 by GCSEs.

18 Certificate of Secondary Education—examinations for the 16+ age range, traditionally pitched at a lower level of ability than O-levels. They were replaced, along with O-levels, by GCSEs—General Certificate of Secondary Education.

19 *Science in the National Curriculum* (London: H.M.S.O., 1989), p. 79.

20 Ibid. p. 36. The italics, which appear in the document itself, indicate that the words italicized constitute non-statutory examples. This was stated by a DES official at a meeting attended by the author in the autumn of 1989.

21 *Science in the National Curriculum*, p. 36.

22 *Science in the National Curriculum* (London: Cassell Education, 1991), p. 22.

23 *Science in the National Curriculum* (London: H.M.S.O., 1995), p. 24.

Towards a biblical education

Christianity and education

It could be argued—rightly in the view of this author—that education in the United Kingdom owes a great deal to the churches. There were, for example, many children in the nineteenth-century who learned to read only because of the Sunday School movement. The strong link between Christianity and education is still visible, albeit in diluted form, in the existence of institutions such as church schools, affiliated to the Church of England or Anglican Church in Wales. The concept is enshrined in law, insofar as education is still seen to be one of the four heads of charity, under existing charity legislation.

Nevertheless, it has become fashionable to speak of 'separating church and state' in our schools. This concept, borrowed from the United States of America,[1] suggests that it is somehow morally wrong to present religion (by which Christianity is usually being meant) to children in the context of any lesson other than religious education. That an appeal to morality can be made by those who hold that there are no absolute values is one thing, but the proposition also ignores that the presentation of a topic divorced from faith is itself a statement of values.

The Bible actually has a great deal to say about education. It says much about training and education generally, as well as some specific pointers to how our children are to be educated. The present discussion will divide these by first examining the general topic of education, concentrating mainly on a study of the first epistle of Paul to Timothy. Then we will proceed to an analysis of what the Bible says about how we are to have our children educated.

The biblical nature of education

Paul, an apostle of Jesus Christ, by the commandment of God our Saviour and the Lord Jesus Christ, our hope, to Timothy, a true son in the faith: Grace, mercy, and peace from God our Father and Jesus Christ our Lord. (1 Timothy 1:1–2)

Paul was Timothy's teacher, in so many ways. Timothy was a young man of mixed background. His mother was Jewish and his father was Greek. Because of his upbringing with his father, he had not been circumcised. Therefore Paul had him circumcised, in order not to offend his Jewish listeners (Acts 16:3), even though Paul did not accept that Christians had to be circumcised (Galatians 2:14–17). So in many ways Paul became like a new father to Timothy, and this is emphasised in Paul's description of Timothy as 'a true son in the faith'. This fact illustrates that in a genuine teacher-pupil relationship there is bound to be much of a father-son element. This point will be expanded further in the next section.

Timothy is not just referred to as a son; he is described as a *true* son. So a true son is one who takes his teaching in the same way as Timothy did. Paul had confidence that Timothy would be able to deliver his teaching in the way that Paul would have done himself. 'For this reason I have sent Timothy to you, who is my beloved and faithful son in the Lord, who will remind you of my ways in Christ, as I teach everywhere in every church' (1 Corinthians 4:17). This is not to say that Timothy's work was always successful. There would appear to have been some problems, when Timothy was ministering in Corinth, as Paul has to remind them 'Let no one despise him (Timothy)' (1 Corinthians 16:11). So the fact that Paul describes Timothy as a true son does not imply any perfection on Timothy's part—it implies that Timothy was diligent in carrying out his ministry in the way he had learned from Paul.

As I urged you when I went into Macedonia—remain in Ephesus that you may charge some that they teach no other doctrine, nor give heed to fables and endless genealogies, which cause disputes rather than godly edification which is in faith (1 Timothy 1:3–4).

The word 'doctrine' means 'teaching'. Paul has taught Timothy to be a teacher. He expects that Timothy will oversee the teaching ministry in Ephesus, and ensure that only correct doctrine is taught. There is a 'teaching cascade' in this verse; the teaching that Paul gave to Timothy, the teaching that Timothy gives to the other teachers in Ephesus, and finally we have the teaching of these teachers to the people. These Ephesian teachers are to be responsible to Timothy, who oversees their doctrine, and ensures its correctness. Timothy is at all times, however, responsible to Paul for his teaching ministry, who in turn is responsible to God.

Good teaching is contrasted with poor teaching. Poor teaching, says Paul, takes the form of fables and endless genealogies. The former is a good description of any type of liberal doctrine. Liberal doctrines, from people who do not have a high regard for the Bible, will inevitably be like fables. There is an impression of meaninglessness about such teachings. The teachings that Paul is anxious to promote are the true teachings of the gospel:

The law is not made for a righteous person, but for the lawless and insubordinate, for the ungodly and for sinners, for the unholy and profane, for murderers of fathers and murderers of mothers, for manslayers, for fornicators, for sodomites, for kidnappers, for liars, for perjurers, and if there is any other thing that is contrary to sound doctrine, according to the glorious gospel of the blessed God which was committed to my trust. (1 Timothy 1:9–11)

At the end of the Epistle, Paul emphasizes this issue of trust. To emphasize the point, the following verse is quoted from both NKJV and KJV.

O Timothy Guard what was committed to your trust, avoiding the profane and idle babblings and contradictions of what is falsely called knowledge. (1 Timothy 6:20, NKJV).

O Timothy, keep that which is committed to thy trust, avoiding profane and vain babblings, and oppositions of science falsely so called. (1 Timothy 6:20, KJV)

The 'sound doctrine' is that which is 'according to the glorious gospel of the blessed God'. This teaching is committed to us as a trust. Paul held the teaching as a trust and charges Timothy so to hold it likewise. The standards of the Bible are therefore not to be treated as optional extras, nor merely as guidelines. They are rather standards, which themselves constitute part of that 'sound doctrine'.

The KJV use of the word 'science' can cause confusion if not carefully handled. some claim that this verse specifically refers to Darwinian evolution. This is not the case. The word translated as 'science' is *gnosis*, which actually means 'knowledge'—hence the translation offered in the NKJV. This is not to imply that the KJV translators got things wrong. At the time that the KJV was produced (1611), the word 'science' actually meant 'knowledge'. This is why we read sometimes that scholars centuries ago would consider theology to be a science. Theology clearly is a science by the 17th century definition of science, being knowledge, but not by the twenty-first-century definition. Nevertheless, it can be pointed out that knowledge *includes* science, so we are to be on our guard against false knowledge, including false science.

The context of the word *gnosis*, in 1 Timothy 6, suggests knowledge in the sense of the Gnostics. Gnosticism, as a heresy, is derived from the Greek *gnosis*, and implies that adherents are in possession of secret knowledge not available to the general public. Gnostic-type errors are still common today. The whole philosophy behind mysterious ideas of Bible coding and numerology seems to be an example of modern Gnosticism. It is not possible for the ordinary plain reading of Scripture to reveal the ideas found with such codes. Yet, as Christians, we maintain that the plain reading of Scripture is usually the correct one, so severe doubts are cast on such teachings. Similar charges of Gnosticism are levelled at the philosophies and ideas behind the successful novel *The Da Vinci Code*,[2] which contains the blasphemous suggestion that Jesus and Mary Magdalene had had a child together, who was the direct ancestor of many European royal families. Also popularised in this novel is the idea that the New Testament, and indeed the rest of the Bible, contains code, usually in the form of numerical equivalents of Hebrew and Greek words, the interpretation of which is available only to those who have the special inside knowledge— hence *Gnosticism*, which claims to be the supposed inside knowledge.

Having stated what we do not learn from the verse, we can now analyse what we *should* learn. What Paul is underlining once again for Timothy is the need to 'guard what was committed to your trust'. The true teaching of the gospel is very important. It is not to be cloaked with so-called 'special knowledge'. Rather it is to be open and honest. Once again, we see that what Paul has taught Timothy is considered to be a trust, because it is the true teaching of the gospel.

To conclude this section, we can deduce the following lessons from Timothy's apprenticeship to Paul.

- The role of teacher to pupil is very similar to that of father to son
- Sound teaching from God's word is considered to be a trust
- This trust is to be guarded well
- This trust is so important that the pupil needs to be reminded of it.

These are principles which can be applied to a properly biblical mode of education. These principles are not necessarily congruent, however, with a contemporary model of liberal education. Liberal education suggests that the learner should be given the knowledge, skills and understanding, but not the values.

Paul's education of Timothy is very different. The father-son relationship implies that the most important aspect of the education is the values. The most important thing that Paul has taught Timothy is the way of salvation. We can conjecture on the other aspects of Paul's syllabus—maybe he has discussed with Timothy about the methodology of preaching. Perhaps after Paul has preached, he has encouraged Timothy to analyse how Paul presented the gospel. Maybe Paul has constructively criticised Timothy's own ministry. Certainly Timothy is being encouraged in turn to criticise the ministry of other church teachers in Ephesus. However, all these skills are secondary in importance to the message of the gospel which Paul, repeatedly emphasises, is to be a trust.

Jones *et al* have summed up the fallacy of value-free education, in the Christian Schools' Trust's excellent handbook, *Science in Faith*.

All this (secular liberalism) is especially clear in schools. Children have to be exposed to all the options. Thus in RE they learn about, e.g. Islam and Hinduism, as well as about Christianity. What, of course, they really learn (the hidden curriculum) is that no option, no religion, has a compelling claim to be treated as true. Their individual choice takes priority. They are placed at the centre of the moral universe. In so far as this education works, our children will be internalising the dogmas of secular liberalism …

There is a strong flavour of deception and bad faith about secular liberalism. In schools, options are actually presented only in certain areas, notably politics, ethics, philosophy and religion. Options are not presented in the mainstream secular subjects, e.g. in science. On the contrary, the total absence of reference to God and faith in the 'secular' curriculum underlines the irrelevance of God to those subjects and undergirds the secular message already received in RE.[3]

One commendable attempt to produce a more Pauline educational model is the Trinity Curriculum Model, developed by David Freeman at the King's School, Oxfordshire. In this model, the Father is seen as the *source* of all things, the Son as the *means*, and the Holy Spirit as the one who leads us towards *fulfilment*. Thus a curriculum plan needs to contain information on source, means and fulfilment. In their book, *Fighting the Secular Giants*, Thomas and Freeman give several examples of the application of this curriculum method. These examples are extended, so the present work only quotes part of one example:—a lesson on the water cycle.

Source
God ... is Jehovah Jireh who provides all the water needed for creation.

Heart concept (the seed truth of wisdom expressed in one sentence):

The Water Cycle reveals God's wise and economic provision ...

Means
How shall I demonstrate the Water Cycle to my students?

Through questions we will assess their prior knowledge about rain and where it originates ... Understanding of change of temperature altering the state of water will be clarified.

Fulfilment
Has the student understood what this means about God? Through discussion or set question we want them to see the implications behind the Water Cycle and heart concept ...

Can we apply the wise and economic provision of God to the 'recycling' of plants through seed reproduction? ...4

The above quote does not tell one everything about a lesson on the water cycle, as to quote the whole account would have taken three pages. Nevertheless, it is hoped that the above quote gives a sufficient flavour to show that a supposed 'secular' topic, namely the water cycle, actually transmits sound biblical values to the student. The more traditional, secular approach also transmits value; the value being that God is detached from his creation. This philosophy is similar to that of those ancient Greeks, known as Epicureans. They held that the gods were far off, and uninvolved in the day-to-day activities of people. This Epicurean philosophy is in contrast to a value-led approach, which emphasises to the student that the important *thrust* is what we understand in the gospel about God.

Biblical education of children

In the above section, we have attempted a general philosophy of education from the Bible. It is soon found, as one looks into the Bible, that specific things are said about the education of children. This section examines a number of key verses, many of which are from the Book of Proverbs.

Train up a child in the way he should go, And when he is old he will not depart from it. (Proverbs 22:6)

The purpose of training children is to set them on the right course for life. In this verse, it is clear that what is being taught is a way of living, rather than knowledge and understanding. Whereas secular liberal education requires content without value, biblical education maintains that the value is more important than the content.

It is not too strong a claim to suggest that the rise in teenage delinquency that so many bemoan is linked in some way to a philosophy that suggests knowledge and understanding require no values. If the children are educated in school to believe that values are incidental, then society should not wonder that they reject values when out of school.

A wise son heeds his father's instruction, But a scoffer does not listen to rebuke. (Proverbs 13:1)

There is a great deal to analyse in this verse. First, it speaks about wisdom. Wisdom is not the same in the Bible as intelligence. Wisdom has a strong moral component.

What is it that makes the son wise? It is that he 'heeds his father's instruction'. The idea of *instruction* as a means of education was frowned upon when the author was at teacher training college. Instead, the teacher was to be a *facilitator*—a sort of resource available to the students who wanted to find things out for themselves. Although there is a case for the teacher being both instructor and facilitator, in practice the extreme of such a philosophy is unworkable, and the teacher ends up guiltily explaining things to the student.

Moreover, the concept of instruction once more suggests that values are important in education. Note that the contrast is with a 'scoffer'. He is one who 'does not listen to rebuke'. Therefore, being rebuked is not in itself a sign of foolishness (the biblical opposite of wisdom). Not listening to the rebuke is what shows lack of wisdom.

Finally, we should note who the teacher is. The teacher happens to be the student's father. This is a very important point, which must not be overlooked.

Surely I have taught you statutes and judgments, just as the LORD my God commanded me, that you should act according to them in the land which you go to possess. Therefore be careful to observe them; for this is your wisdom and your understanding in the sight of the peoples who will hear all these statutes, and say, 'Surely this great nation is a wise and understanding people.' For what great nation is there that has God so near to it, as the LORD our God is to us, for whatever reason we may call upon Him? And what great nation is there that has such statutes and righteous judgments as are in all this law which I set before you this day? Only take heed to yourself, and diligently keep yourself, lest you forget the things your eyes have seen, and lest they depart from your heart all the days of your life. *And teach them to your children and your grandchildren,* especially concerning the day you stood before the LORD your God in Horeb, when the LORD said to me, 'Gather the people to Me, and I will let them hear My words, that they may learn to fear Me all the days they live on the earth, and *that they may teach their children.*' (Deuteronomy 4:5–10) [emphasis mine]

The passage is quoted at length, so that the context can be observed. However, this study will concentrate on the emphasised sections. The Lord is commanding the people to teach something to their children and grandchildren. What they are supposed to be teaching is, once again, a matter of values. They are to be taught the 'statutes and judgements' of God. It is clear that the beginning of education is the word of God. It is a matter of training our children to see the world, and everything in it, through the 'spectacles' of the Bible. Nor is this responsibility only for one generation. The children in turn are to train their children, but there is also the need to train the grandchildren. Thus, no child should be overlooked.

It cannot escape our notice that in every case in the Bible, education is seen as a family generational issue. We are to train our children. Specifically, it is fathers who are to train their children. In a family context, the education that a child receives must be from the parent. If the parent is unable to deliver that education themselves, then they must have complete confidence in those carrying out the education on their behalf. We must study this further from another passage.

Hear, O Israel: The LORD our God, the LORD is one You shall love the LORD your God with all your heart, with all your soul, and with all your strength. And these words which I command you today shall be in your heart. *You shall teach them diligently to your children,* and shall talk of them when you sit in your house, when you walk by the way, when you lie down, and when you rise up. (Deuteronomy 6:4–7) [emphasis mine]

In this passage, we read the commandment which Jesus describes in Matthew 22:37 as 'the greatest commandment'. This commandment is itself something that we should teach to our children.

Notice the means of teaching. The teaching is to be done diligently. It is to be done by regular conversation, while relaxing in the lounge, while walking to work and school, and at bedtime and when waking your children, if the passage may be paraphrased slightly.

Notice once again who is doing the teaching. It is the parents. We teach *our* children, not children in general.

Notice the substance of the command. We are to love God with all our *heart, soul* and *strength.* To the Hebrew way of thinking, the heart was the seat of the intellect. Thus it is to do with the knowledge and understanding of the child being taught. The soul perhaps implies our worship, and our strength implies that everything about us physically and mentally is to love God with all we have.

When we consider, once again, that education is the prerogative of the parent, we need to consider how this may be practically achieved.

One method, very legitimate and praiseworthy, is for the children to be home-schooled. This is a growing phenomenon in the UK, and is not, in fact, confined to Christian homes. Indeed, the majority of home-schoolers in the UK are non-Christian families. There are organisations that have been set up to aid in home-schooling, providing curricula and advice for parents. Nevertheless, there will be many parents who feel unable to live up to this ideal. This does not excuse the parents from their responsibility to educate their children, but this responsibility can be delegated. The contentious issue is: to whom will the parents delegate the responsibility? It is increasingly the opinion of this author, that it can be inappropriate to delegate this responsibility to a secular, state school, where the values proclaimed are so alien to the Christian biblical values of the home. This issue will be expanded further in later chapters. For the moment, it should be noted that Christian parents need to do what they feel able to do. This will involve different levels of response. For example, there may be those who want to home-school their children, but find that circumstances prevent it. There will be others who feel able to work with the state system, as they feel they have opportunity to be of influence and benefit within it.

It is encouraging to note that there are an increasing number of independent Christian schools in the UK, governed by parents, run along biblical and family lines. Such schools, complying with all the necessary legislation in the UK, can often be a pragmatic way for Christian parents to fulfil their responsibility for the education of their children. Many readers, whose children are in state schools, may profoundly disagree with this analysis, but it is not an analysis that can be ignored. Certainly, Christians who send their children to state schools need to find other ways to be thoroughly involved in the education of their children. Do you know the people to whom you have delegated the teaching of your precious children? Do you know what philosophy your children are being indoctrinated with?

Later in the book, we will examine the myth of neutrality. It must be emphasised at this point, however, that text books and school courses are not neutral. As Ken Ham has said, 'If the text books don't start with the Bible as foundational to their thinking, then they are secular in philosophy.'⁵ Or, as Jesus put it more bluntly, 'He who is not with Me is against Me, and he who does not gather with Me scatters abroad' (Matthew 12:30).

It has been suggested that children of Christian parents need to be in state schools in order to be salt and light. This ignores the fact that the children concerned may not yet be saved, and may certainly not yet be mature enough to take on the world. There is a strong case for our children to be protected.

When Jesus spoke about salt, he said, 'You are the salt of the earth; but if the salt loses its flavour, how shall it be seasoned? It is then good for nothing but to be thrown out and trampled underfoot by men' (Matthew 5:13). In New Testament times, salt could lose its flavour by contamination. Unscrupulous dealers might cut the salt with bland materials such as limestone or even sand. Eventually, after this had been done a few times, the salt became worthless and had to be thrown out. Children, at a formative stage of development, should not be filled with contaminated salt.

In fact, the Bible at no point sanctions the state to educate our children. As has been observed, education is the preserve and the duty of the parent; specifically, the father. A characteristic of children is that they can be easily influenced (Ephesians 4:14). It would seem right for Christian parents to ensure that their children come under positive influences in all aspects of their curriculum.

'Do not learn the way of the Gentiles,' says Jeremiah (Jeremiah 10:2). If there is a philosophy being taught to our children, which is opposed to what the Bible is teaching, then we need to examine what that philosophy teaches.

Notes

1 American readers will note that many have observed that the notion of separation of 'church

and state' in education is, in fact, based on an erroneous interpretation of the First Amendment to the US Constitution. See, for example, **F. A. Schaeffer,** *A Christian Manifesto* (Westchester, IL: Crossway, 1981), p. 109ff.

2 **D. Brown,** *The Da Vinci Code* (London: Corgi, 2004).

3 Christian Schools' Trust Science Curriculum Team, *Science in Faith* (CST, 1998), p. 12.

4 These are very brief excerpts from **S. Thomas** and **D. Freeman,** *Fighting the Secular Giants* (Oxfordshire Community Churches, 2001) pp. 99–108.

5 From *Raising Godly Children in an Ungodly World*, a DVD issued by Answers in Genesis.

Spirituality and science

A spiritual universe

The night sky has always inspired a sense of awe. Children are endlessly fascinated by what they can see. As they try, in vain, to count the number of little bright pin-pricks of light above them, the teacher, if they can adequately lead the children into a greater understanding of the universe, is at a great advantage.

As a small boy, I was fascinated by the night sky. My father and I would spend hours looking at it, with a small telescope and pair of binoculars. As I learned to read, I began to read books about astronomy. I met a famous astronomer, who taught me the names of some stars, and how to find them. The more I knew, the more I loved the sky.

It has been estimated that there are 10^{22} stars in the universe. 10^{22} is a very big number. It is a 1 with 22 noughts after it.

10,000,000,000,000,000,000,000

Interestingly, a typical beach has about the same number of grains of sand.[1] These two concepts are compared with each other in Genesis, the book which stands first in both the Hebrew and Christian views of divine revelation: 'Blessing I will bless you, and multiplying I will multiply your descendants as the stars of the heaven and as the sand which is on the seashore; and your descendants shall possess the gate of their enemies (Genesis 22:17).

While the number of stars visible to the naked eye in the sky is only in the order of a few thousand, the figure of 10^{22} is achieved only when one calculates the number of stars in our galaxy and the number of galaxies in the universe. These facts coincide neatly for the purpose of this study, as we develop a fuller understanding of spiritual thinking. Scientists have also estimated that the number of nerve signal transmissions or impulses in the brain is also of the order of 10^{22}, while others have suggested that there is a sense in which this human organ carries an innate analogy of the cosmos in its processes. While it would be incorrect to draw spurious conclusions based on the coincidence of these numbers, they may serve to illustrate the fascination that there is in linking the scientific with the spiritual. At the very least, I would suggest that it is interesting that the Bible compares the number of stars in the heavens to the number of grains of sand on the beach, when the number is so vast—and so vastly more than the number of stars that can actually be seen with the naked eye.

At this point in the discussion, the science educator must pay attention to the word *spiritual*, which Collins dictionary defines as 'pertaining to spirit or mind; not material; unworldly; pertaining to sacred things; holy'. Much contemporary interest in issues such as the environment and so-called New Age thinking underlines a desire on the part of people today to seek after things spiritual.[2] *The Illustrated Bible Dictionary* suggests that the idea of spirit is conveyed in the Hebrew word *rûah* and the Greek word πνευμα (*pneuma*).[3] Both words convey the sense of wind or breath. In the Old Testament context, *rûah* often implies something that happens not explicable by naturalistic means:

At its heart is the *experience* of a mysterious, awesome power—the mighty invisible force of the wind, the mystery of vitality, the otherly power that transforms—all *rûah*, all manifestations of divine power.[4]

However, in the New Testament, more is made of the *personal* characteristics of πνευμα, though this interpretation is not absent from the Old Testament expression, and *The Illustrated Bible Dictionary* states:

It is important to realise that for the first Christians the Spirit was thought of in terms of divine power clearly manifest by its effects on the life of the recipient; the impact of the Spirit did not leave individual or onlooker in much doubt that a significant change had taken place by divine agency.[5]

While different people might understand the concept of 'divine agency' differently, it is a sufficiently inclusive term to enable progress to be made in the understanding of this spiritual dimension of the universe, for the present purpose. The practical outworking of the issues raised here is that a personal view of the universe can embrace both the spiritual and the scientific dimension of human understanding. There is no dichotomy between belief in the Bible and the practice of correct scientific methodology. Nevertheless, such a dichotomy has been assumed in the UK education system, to the detriment of students' education in science.

The spiritual dimension of science in the National Curriculum

Schools have sometimes been compared mischievously to assembly lines. The pupils arrive at the school as raw materials. They travel along the conveyer belt of the daily timetable. When they reach the classrooms, the teachers do their educating on the children, much as an assembly line worker might do some welding on a car. At one stop the pupils have some maths done on them. The bell goes and they move on to have some geography done on them. Eventually they reach the end of the conveyer belt, where they undergo some quality control tests (GCSEs or A-Levels) and the finished product (an educated pupil) is sold to the customer (society, or possibly, the world of work).

Such a mechanical view of school life allows for little interplay between the various subjects in the curriculum. It would imply that science is science, and religion is for RE or assemblies. There is no suggestion—indeed the opposite is implied—that there might be any link between these curriculum areas, even though there are contemporary trends toward the development of cross-curricular themes. As a result, schools often reinforce the popular misconception that science and spirituality are mutually exclusive. Scientists themselves are often to blame for this state of affairs, which is perpetuated by the media and the purveyors of popular science. For example, the author was involved in a discussion for a television show pilot. My opponent, a science journalist, came out with the old chestnut 'Religious faith has no place in the science classroom'. It was actually the programme anchor who responded, 'Why not?' and the science journalist was momentarily flummoxed. The divorce between science and spirituality, which has developed in the West, emerged from nineteenth-century positivism. Its promulgators were looking for a new definition of science, in which God was not needed. Colin Chant is a senior lecturer with the Open University. He explained:

First, there arose among practising scientists, a conviction that their investigations needed to be liberated from preconceptions, which were metaphysical either in origin or import. They held that so long as their colleagues were interested in upholding or in combating particular metaphysical positions, scientific inquiry could not be free.[6]

Richard Dawkins, Simonyi Professor for the Public Understanding of Science at Oxford University, is one of the best known opponents of the spiritual dimension of science, and therefore he pours scorn on those who ask the question 'why?' of scientists, whom he claims are used to answering only the question 'how?'

You have no right to assume that the 'Why?' question deserves an answer when posed about a boulder, a misfortune, Mt. Everest or the universe. Questions can be simply inappropriate, however heartfelt their framing.[7]

Dawkins's views, usually regarded by many as extreme, are hardly free from bias. Indeed, Alister McGrath, Professor of Historical Theology at the same Oxford University, who has a PhD in molecular biophysics, says:

To put it bluntly, Dawkins' engagement with theology is superficial and inaccurate, often amounting to little more than cheap point scoring … His tendency to misrepresent the views of his opponents is the least attractive aspect of his writings.[8]

Moreover, the question 'why?' was not intended to be the purpose behind the National Curriculum, yet the second edition of the document, *Science in the National Curriculum* (1991), contained the following comment, which we have noted before:

Pupils should be given opportunities to develop their knowledge and understanding of how scientific ideas change through time and how their nature and the use to which they are put are affected by the social, moral, *spiritual*, and cultural contexts in which they are developed.[9]

Much literature has been produced on teaching the social implications of science, putting science into context and into everyday life, which could help in the development of such opportunities. Titles of published *schemes of work*[10] frequently reflect the extent of this work: e.g. 'Science at Work' or 'Science and Technology in Society'.[11] If they are examined, it will be seen how discussions in science lessons have featured moral issues, of which the problems associated with global warming, nuclear energy or the ozone layer are excellent examples. But the 'spiritual implications of science' and how they are to be taught have not yet figured in recent debate. During the time that the author was a head of science (1996–1999), he received regular catalogues of text books from major educational publishers (e.g. Heinemann, Collins or Oxford), not one of which contained material for pupils, to help them learn about science in a spiritual context. It is hoped that this present study will provide a contribution towards filling this gap.

The supposed dichotomy

The view that science and spirituality are opposed is widespread and there can indeed sometimes be an impression that science has done away with the need for spirituality. This thinking is basic to the arguments promoted by Dawkins, who has achieved prominence in recent years as a principal controversialist in the field between science and religion. He denigrates many essentially religious questions as being 'simply inappropriate.'[12] His attitude has been emboldened by the extraordinarily timid manner adopted by many spiritual leaders in the dialogue between science and spirituality, since Bishop Wilberforces's ill-fated debates with Thomas Huxley (often referred to as 'Darwin's Bulldog') in the 1850s. The impression is sometimes given that humankind has outgrown the need for spirituality and religion as we start the twenty-first century.

In order to illustrate the medieval approach to the relationship between science and faith, as far as they were able to understand either, I have quoted below from works of medieval mystics Julian of Norwich and Meister Eckhart. I cannot describe their views as being in any way biblical, or Christian. Nevertheless, it was important for the purposes of the original Master's dissertation, on which this work is based, to refer to such medieval thought. I am not recommending that readers would be edified by studying their works, but their comments are of use to us, to understand how Western views of separation of church and state developed.

The ancient fourteenth-century hermit and mystic, Mother Julian of Norwich, had a fascinating insight into the relationship between God and nature, as she sat in her 'hermitage', propped against St Julian's Church in Norwich. One could almost describe this as a scientific insight. In one of her 'visions', she saw:

Something small, about the size of a hazelnut ... seemed to lie in the palm of my hand as round as a tiny ball. I tried to understand the sight of it, wondering what it could possibly mean. The answer came: 'This is all that is made.'[13]

It is not that Julian's view of the universe was small, but rather that her view of God was big. Julian is seeing the totality of the universe in the context of a unified vision and it is precisely this insight which underlines the claims for the profound spirituality of science, which follow when the human mind and the containing cosmos are seen as having a common purpose. Her vision of creation troubled her.

I felt it was so small that it could easily fade to nothing; but again I was told: 'This lasts and it will go on lasting forever because God loves it. And it is so with every being that God loves.'[14]

It could be argued that Julian's scientific knowledge would be rudimentary, even by the standards of the time, but that in itself is not the issue. The point is that Julian can be understood as having seen a link between things material, as she perceives them, and things spiritual. Indeed, in her times the notion that there was some separation between things spiritual and temporal would have been difficult to comprehend.

Another medieval mystic, who also took this mystical approach to his view of the universe, was Meister Eckhart. Eckhart, born in Erfurt, Thuringia in 1260, was a disciple of Thomas Aquinas's ideas, discussed later in this chapter. He drew heavily on mythic imagery in his writings. He believed that the things he saw around him—what he called 'external creatures'—were to be perceived spiritually. He says that it is our souls which take notice of the universe. In particular, this is achieved when the soul allows God to enter into it.

When the agents of the soul contact creatures, they take and make ideas and likenesses of them and bear them back again into the self. It is by means of these ideas that the soul knows about external creatures. Creatures cannot approach the soul except in this way and the soul cannot get at creatures, except on its own initiative, unless it first conceives ideas of them. Thus the soul gets at things by means of ideas and the idea is an entity created by the soul's agents. Be it a stone, or a rose, or a person, or whatever it is that is to be known, first an idea is taken and then absorbed, and in this way the soul connects with the phenomenal world.[15]

It will seem odd to evangelicals that I am taking time to quote such mystics as Julian and Eckhart. Indeed, their view of nature is difficult for modern minds to comprehend. It must be emphasised that my purpose in quoting them is not to endorse their ideas—there is much in the Eckhart quote above that reads almost as occultist. My purpose is to illustrate that in all the development of thought down the ages, on issues pertaining to science, there has never been, until comparatively recently, a concept of compartmentalisation of the curriculum disciplines. For example, both Julian and Eckhart are touching on areas which today would be the preserve of science. It is nevertheless natural for them to relate these areas to their ideas of God.

In Eckhart, for example, the idea that objects have their being because of their interaction with the observer's soul is encompassed by modern cognitive psychology, in recognition of the precedence of consciousness in our interpretation of reality. In essence, the argument is parallel with the old question which asks if a table in a room still exists when the light is out. The issue of whether the table still exists or not is, in a sense, irrelevant, because it is literally beyond the observer's experience. However, Eckhart makes a link between our understanding of nature and science and our understanding of God. Education, in much the same way, links its acknowledgement of the child's abilities with the whole field of its potential. It is the task of the scientific disciplines to encourage humans to perceive that world objectively in a meaningful way, but definitions of spirituality so far examined need to be expanded.

Schaeffer has a comment on this.

The areas of true Spirituality ... are not basically external; they are internal, they are deep ... The internal is the basic; the external is merely the result.[16]

This is important, because it touches on the heart of the supposed dichotomy; the idea that the recognition of spirituality, by its presence in the educational debate, addresses individual perceptions of the universe, whereas the place of science in the curriculum is concerned to enable the pupil to comprehend and to deal with objective perceptions. While it will be shown later that science is equally as subjective as spirituality, this direction of the discussion will not differ with Schaeffer's assumption that spirituality is internal. Spirituality deals with the implicit order, while science deals with the explicit. Both are complementary, if the pupil is to be awakened to the whole of reality.

This should not be taken to be as if this author believes that spirituality is purely subjective, with no objective base. On the contrary. Dawkins has defined faith, believing it to be entirely subjective, as follows:

Faith means blind trust, in the absence of evidence, even in the teeth of evidence.[17]

McGrath is scathing about Dawkins' definition of faith.

So what is the evidence that anyone—let alone religious people—defines 'faith' in this absurd way? The simple fact is that Dawkins offers no defence of this definition, which bears little relation to any religious (or any other) sense of the word.... It is Dawkins' own definition, constructed with his own agenda in mind, being represented as if it were characteristic of those he wishes to criticize.[18]

The Bible gives a much more succinct definition of faith, implying that it is, in fact, an objective quality.

Now faith is the substance of things hoped for, the evidence of things not seen. For by it the elders obtained a good testimony. By faith we understand that the worlds were framed by the word of God, so that the things which are seen were not made of things which are visible (Hebrews 11:1–3).

The writer to the Hebrews points to the evidential nature of faith. Creationist speaker Carl Kerby has a talk entitled 'What is the best evidence for creation?', showing that, despite many very, very strong evidences for creation, the best evidence that God created is, in fact, the word of God itself. The Bible is believed by faith and this faith, in itself, has the characteristic of objective evidence. The NIV translation of Hebrews 11:1 uses the word 'certain'. 'Faith is being sure of what we hope for and certain of what we do not see.'

The world and the universe are seen through human eyes. What is seen is personal to the observer and cannot accurately be reproduced for any other individual, yet there is another sense in which the perception of the individual is 'learned', as the raw data of our senses is 'trained' by being explained within the scientific paradigm. Although a person's relationship with God is itself personal and peculiar to the individual concerned, the generalities of such a relationship are not, and can be communicated by practice and teaching. If this were not so, there would be no market for devotional works. Such generalities take their shape, to have their meaning, in the mind of the individual. The educationalist's task of relating the subject's abilities to their potential, private experience with public knowledge is relevant to our understanding of the process.

Cheslyn Jones, former principal of Pusey House, Oxford, has also emphasised this individuality of spiritual experience. 'I have a unique responsibility before him (i.e. the other) which cannot be delegated to any other being.'[19] A Sunday School chorus suggests similarly, 'There's a work for Jesus (that) none but *you* can do.' Jones has examined a number of passages from Scripture to support his claim. In one example, he discusses the apostle Paul's statement in 1 Timothy 1:15: 'This is a faithful saying and worthy of all acceptance, that Christ Jesus came into the world to save sinners, *of whom I am chief*' (emphasis mine). The apostle Paul understood that his relationship with God is as an individual. It has to apply directly to him. He explains further that he sees this individual relationship as eternal and final, quoting 2 Corinthians 5:10, 'For we must all appear before the judgement seat of Christ, that each one may receive *the things done in the body, according to what he has done, whether good or bad*' (emphasis mine). It is a view of spirituality which is clearly personal and related to the individual's own historical personal experience and attitude. However, this spirituality is not only individual and subjective. It is complemented by such statements as 1 Corinthians 12:13: 'For by one Spirit we were all baptized into one body—whether Jews or Greeks, whether slaves or free—and *have all been made to drink into one Spirit*' (emphasis mine). This is an expression of *corporate spirituality*.

These theological explorations may seem to be at a distance from educational techniques, but they reflect a complementary aspect of the human process of recognition and the construction of meaning, both of which are individual *and* corporate. The distinctive formulation is specifically Christian, but has wide implications. We shall need to follow these implications through, but we can begin to explore them by recalling that Calvin designated the schoolteacher as a minister of the Christian community, standing in order only a little below the presbyter—the term is a transliteration of the Greek word for elder, and is often used in *presbyterian* churches. The significance of this proximity is that both the presbyter and schoolteacher have a common function in linking individual understanding to the common social order, and Jones helps our understanding of spirituality in this context when he discusses what he terms 'liturgical mysticism'. He defines this as follows:

The liturgical mystic is rather one who in some way distances himself from the corporate action in order to concentrate on its inner or deeper meaning.[20]

Even in the middle of what might be seen as a group activity, namely liturgical worship, Jones shows that the important relationship is that between the individual, who has become the 'mystic', and God. Liturgical worship is highly organised. If all that are present are following a form of words in a service book, which is identical for each participant, there might seem no room for individuality. This is not the case, argues Jones, because all must respond in an individual way to what is going on. Spirituality, in education or in the Christian community, is the quality which recognises 'what is going on'.

Jones develops his idea of mysticism into prayer, which he sees as an expression of spirituality. He describes what he calls 'mystical prayer' as the 'higher stages of prayer'.[21] Here Jones seems to suggest that the individual's spirituality in his personal prayers brings him closer to God. This strange view is alien to those of us within the Bible-believing, evangelical tradition, but it is mentioned here, only because Jones is arguing that this anchors spirituality within a rational and objective context. He claims support from Augustine's emotional prayer.

In the place where I had been angry with myself, within my chamber where I felt the pang of penitence, where I had made a sacrifice offering up my old life and placing my hope in you as I first began to meditate on my renewal: there you began to be my delight, and you gave 'gladness in my heart'. And I cried out loud when I acknowledged inwardly what I read in external words.[22]

While this author would see the above quote in terms of Augustine's repentance, I would agree that the experience described is of objective reality. The emotion of the event does not in any way detract from the fact that it happened.

The educationalist may well see this sort of experience as being just subjective, and therefore of no relevance to the science classroom. Nevertheless, the religious imagination will find this experience as reflecting the meeting of the individual with *reality*, and Jones, in examining the phenomenon, suggests that such an outpouring of individual emotional spirituality can mix with that of others, leading to a corporate or 'interpersonal mysticism'.[23] This *common* experience might compare with that which can happen to the subject at the 'Last Night of the Proms', during the collective singing of 'Rule Britannia', or during the singing of the 'Star Spangled Banner' during the Super Bowl, or, more pertinently to this author, the singing of 'Mae Hen Wlad fy Nhadau' at the Millennium Stadium The context is different, but the author had an experience, as a teenager, when first participating with that portion of the Anglican liturgy where all say, 'Christ has died Christ is risen Christ will come again ' The ancient words sent a shiver of recognition as they reverberated through the enormous building. The author would argue there was an objective reality in the experience, even though he had not, at that time, become a Christian. Was Archimedes not equally thrilled with recognition when he shouted, 'Eureka ' and are not all these experiences comparable with what the pupil feels when he acknowledges, 'Now I see '?

Edward Yarnold, former tutor in theology at Campion Hall, Oxford, has linked his view of the nature of God with his view of the nature of humanity, and, by implication, for the purposes of this study, with the nature of scientific enquiry. His syllogism is as follows:

- It is God's nature to create
- Human beings are made in the image of God
- Therefore it is human nature to create

Yarnold's syllogism reflects the entirely practical outcome of religious recognition.[24] This link is made in the first chapter of Genesis: 'Then God blessed them, and God said to them, "Be fruitful and multiply; fill the earth and subdue it; have dominion over the fish of the sea, over the birds of the air, and over every living thing that moves on the earth"' (Genesis 1:28).

That great evangelical philosopher, Francis Schaeffer notes the importance of the word 'dominion' (some English translations use the less satisfactory 'rule'), an idea which implies a cultural or scientific mandate.

It isn't that man is simply stronger; as a matter of fact, he isn't always stronger. Dominion itself is an aspect of the image of God in the sense that man, being created in the image of God, stands between God and all which God chose to put under man. As that which was created, man is no higher than all that has been created, but as created in the image of God he has the responsibility to consciously care for all that which God put in his care.[25]

Schaeffer is showing that a link is being forged between the human desire for science and the spiritual dimension. This link is at the heart of the cultural mandate, and indeed is what the mandate is all about. In the broadest possible sense, it explains why science flourished in 'Christian'

Europe. A belief in God, who created the universe and set the universe's laws in place, leads one to suppose that the universe is knowable and therefore worthy of study. For example, some opponents of creationism have suggested that we believe that God put fossils in the rocks as a sort of trick, to test our faith. Nothing could be further from the truth A Christian worldview would never have fostered such nonsense. A Christian worldview expects that, even if we do not yet know the rational answer for something, then that answer must still exist, because God is supremely rational. The 'fossil trick' philosophy was evident in ancient Greece, because their gods were capricious and unpredictable—unlike the Lord God Almighty of the Bible.

Meister Eckhart propounded a philosophy, which suggested that God is 'disinterested'.

Bear in mind also that God has been immovably disinterested from the beginning and still is and that his creation of the heavens and the earth affected him as little as if he had not made a single creature.[26]

However, this notion of disinterest was not meant to imply a lack of concern, the phrase *von Abgescheidenheit* being difficult to match in English, as its meaning falls somewhere between disinterest and detachment.[27] Nevertheless, Blakney, the translator of Eckhart's work, points out that there is a certain coldness that comes across when Eckhart says:

… I go further. All the prayers a man may offer and good works he may do will affect the disinterested God as little as if there were neither prayers nor works, nor will God be any more compassionate or stoop down to man any more because of his prayers and works than if they were omitted.[28]

Eckhart's philosophy of the disinterest of God is depressing, and out of tune with the God of the Bible. Contrast this with the warm, almost conversational nature of Julian's writing, discussed earlier and which is probably more characteristic of a much wider swathe of Christian expression. Schaeffer also reflects this warmer approach in his book *True*

Chapter 3

Spirituality, and gives the opinion that spirituality is about a personal relationship with a personal Holy Spirit.

> The Holy Spirit is a Person, but knowing that He is a Person should remind us that He can be grieved, that He can be made sad.[29]

Schaeffer's focus also helps our thesis, as he says that this personal relationship is exemplified in our ability to create.

> We think and through our bodies we can bring forth into the external world. It can be said that it is impossible for men not to create things constantly and truly.[30]

Schaeffer describes this ability to create as following from our creation in the image of God.

> The internal thought-world is first, and the internal thought-world causes the external. This should not surprise us, because we have been made in the image of God, and so are rational and moral. Putting these elements together, we find: God thinks, and then God brings forth into the external world, which He had originally created out of nothing; we think, and we bring forth into the external world.[31]

Three conclusions can be drawn from these comments.
- First, that spirituality and science are ways of trying to interpret the universe and they have for many centuries been seen as such, and as complementary to each other. They are not hostile to each other.
- Second, that spirituality and science are linked in the minds of many thinkers. While others may reject such a link, it has been the purpose of this section, not to prove a link, but to demonstrate that acceptance of such a link is a legitimate position to hold.
- Third, that spirituality can be seen in terms of an individual's response to the universe or to God or to both at one and the same time. It can also be understood as a collective response to both. Science is a societal response to the universe. This is not to suppose that it is non-individual in its import, nor to say that it is a view of the universe that excludes God, or an individual, or a collective relationship with God.

There is a view of science in which one's understanding of the universe depends on one's position as observer within it. This is a viewpoint which need neither include nor exclude a religious perspective.

Linguistically, the word 'spiritual' suggests that it can be used as a comparative adjective; i.e. A is 'more spiritual' than B. Its usage can also imply that 'spirituality' is a quality that can be acquired; e.g. A now has a spirituality. These concepts fit happily with the ideas already discussed, and so a fuller definition of spirituality seems to be needed. From this perspective, it is perhaps helpful to suggest that spirituality can be seen as a measure of one's pilgrimage along the road, a measure of personal progress, which is mapped out by one's philosophy, religion or worldview. While there are collective expressions of the ideal (e.g. 'evangelical spirituality') spirituality usually describes an inward experience of the soul.

Science without religion

Religion and science were not always held apart, as they have tended to be in the modern world. However, the present tendency to separate their assumptions goes back a long time and it can even be asserted that Thomas Aquinas paved the way for science without God. This would no doubt have seemed odd to Aquinas himself, because he was a theologian, but Schaeffer has shown that Aquinas's ideas gave rise, as time passed, to the separation between things spiritual and secular.[32] It is characteristic of Aquinian thought that he viewed the universe as having two realms, nature and grace. Nature was the realm of created things, whereas grace was the realm of God and heavenly things. Nature was capable of being understood, so the whole power of the intellect could be brought to bear on it. Grace could not be fully understood and therefore it did not seem correct to try. It is helpful to express this diagrammatically, and this separation can be represented by figure 1. This diagram can be more fully expressed in figure 2, taken from Schaeffer.

Grace
———————
Nature

Figure 1 'Grace beyond nature'[33]

Grace, the higher	*God the creator* of heaven and heavenly things, the unseen and its influence on the earth; *unity* or universals or absolutes which give existence and morals meaning
Nature, the lower	*The created*; earth and earthly things; the visible and what happens normally in the cause-and-effect universe; what man as man does on the earth; *diversity*, or individual things, the participants, or the individual acts of man.

Figure 2[34]

'The Two Realms and their attributes'

It is no exaggeration to say that Aquinas's model of the universe had a profound and overwhelming influence in his own time and has influenced Western thought right up to the present day. He believed that intellectual research should be confined to nature, which is where it has largely stayed. He thought that the upper storey was too wonderful to explore, other than via the paths of liturgy and contemplation.

Hence in the last resort all that man knows of God is to know that he does not know him, since he knows that what God is surpasses all that we can understand of him.[35]

But this lack of exploration today has led to its neglect, and is responsible for the notions of a dichotomy between science and spirituality, or the erroneous ideas of separation between church and state popular in both the USA and UK. Schaeffer describes how intellectual argument has, largely, begun in the lower storey.[36] He believes that this has left no firm foundation for a study of morals. An explosion in activity in the lower storey in the modern era, with science and philosophy, has left most discussion unaware of the upper storey. This attitude would seem to be similar to that expressed today, for example in the common restriction: 'I don't discuss religion or politics.'

Aquinas thought that an argument beginning in the lower storey could embrace the upper. He, therefore, offered proofs for the existence of God, in the following sequence:

- Aristotle's argument for a Prime Mover.
- A similar 'proof' which maintains that as there cannot be an infinite series of causes, there must have been a beginning.

- The argument from contingency, first propounded by the Muslim scholar Ibn Sina, which demands the existence of a 'Necessary Being'.
- Aristotle's argument from the *Philosophy* that the hierarchy of excellence in this world implies a Perfection that is the best of all.
- The argument from design, which maintains that the order and purpose that we see in the universe cannot simply be the result of chance.[37]

However, these arguments are not universally accepted, and Karen Armstrong, unconvinced by these 'proofs', argues: 'Each proof tacitly implies that "God" is simply another being, one more link in the chain of existence.'[38] If one creates a god from 'lower storey arguments' it will turn out that this god is simply a 'lower storey god'. C. S. Lewis explained the implications of this in his description of the difference between Nature and Supernature in his book *Miracles*—a discussion which reflects a sort of neo-Aquinianism:

Naturalism, without ceasing to be itself, could admit a certain kind of God. The great interlocking event called Nature might be such as to produce at some stage a great cosmic consciousness; an indwelling 'God' arising from the whole process as human mind arises (according to the Naturalists) from human organisms. A Naturalist would not object to that sort of God. The reason is this. Such a God would not stand outside Nature or the total system, would not be existing 'on his own'.[39]

Such theories of God have been constructed. This is the kind of 'god' acceptable to physicists like Tipler, whose theories suggest a convergence point for all space, time and mass, which he calls the 'Omega Point'. This Omega Point, once conceived in this way, then takes on the attributes of God.

The logically necessary histories collectively comprising the whole of reality can be regarded as 'emanating' from the Omega Point in his/her transcendence.[40]

It will be observed by fellow evangelicals that this type of god is not at all the God revealed to us in the Bible. Omega Points or naturalistic gods do not display personality, real transcendence, omnipotence, love, grace or wrath. Nor do they display creativity. They are in no wise equivalent to the one true God who we know and worship. Nevertheless, for the moment we will pursue the arguments of these Aquinians to see how Western society's concepts of God and science have developed, and how this affects the sort of science prescribed in the UK's National Curriculum.

It was the philosophical 'enlightenment' of the eighteenth century which exploded the tension in Aquinas' thought, but its thinking did not necessarily dispose of God. Many Enlightenment thinkers believed in God and the attempts of the French Revolution to dispense with the Christian God by the worship of the 'supreme being' are notorious. Rather their arguments began not to *require* God. Karen Armstrong—a prolific writer on comparative religion, and scourge of conservative Christian views—reminds us that Descartes, the most prominent scientific thinker of the age, 'was always careful to submit himself to the rulings of the Roman Catholic Church and saw himself as an orthodox Christian'. Nevertheless, 'the God of Descartes ... was the God of the philosophers who took no cognisance of earthly events'.[41] The background to scientific discussion today is not one of Judaeo-Christian ethics. This is because the upper storey, grace, has been removed. Science without God has come to be considered axiomatic by many people in the Western world who, as Armstrong often reminds us, 'take it for granted that modern cosmology has dealt a death-blow to the idea of God'.[42]

This project of deconstruction has been developed with the support of modern psychology. Freud also took this idea up. He can be described as having been almost religious in his love of science, exclaiming:

No, our science is not an illusion An illusion it would be to suppose that what science cannot give we can get elsewhere.[43]

There is no room in Freud's thinking for God. Indeed, he even told us that he had a new god, when he proposed:

Science, the new *logos*, could take God's place. It could provide a new basis for morality and help us to face our fears.[44]

While his thrust in this direction was modified to some extent by Carl Jung's affirmation of 'God', the Jungian god is too much a reflection of human depth psychology for the modern world to use his proposals as a way back to the God of the Bible. The behavioural sciences generally, rooted in the positivist ideas of the nineteenth century, are almost uniformly structured in a way which confirms the belief in the ultimate infallibility of science. This would now appear to be the prevailing philosophy of the age. This popular philosophy may not suggest that scientists never make sense, but nevertheless assumes that further scientific research will eventually overcome those mistakes, as we continue on the road of scientific progress. It is this confident view which seems to be embedded in the statements of the National Curriculum on these matters.

To quote Armstrong again:

The study of history was dominated by a new myth: that of Progress. It achieved great things but now that damage to the environment has made us realise that this way of life is as vulnerable as the old, we are, perhaps, beginning to realise that it is as fictitious as most of the other mythologies that have inspired humanity over the centuries.[45]

It is before this backdrop that the popularisers of science now stand. Perhaps it is to oversimplify, but the popularisation of science can be described as the New Physics, an approach typified by the work of Stephen Hawking, and the New Biology, which is typified by Richard Dawkins' publications. The present study will attempt to examine some of the popularization pertaining to the New Physics.

Notes

1 Approximate figures discussed in **J. Redid,** *God, the Atom and the Universe* (Grand Rapids: Zondervan, 1968), pp. 74–80.

2 See, for example, **J. Updike,** *Confessions of a Churchgoer*, in *The Guardian,* Saturday 8 January 2000.

3 The *Illustrated Bible Dictionary* (Leicester: Inter-Varsity Press, 1980).

4 Ibid. p. 1479.

5 Ibid. p. 1482.

6   **C. Chant** and **J. Fauvel,** eds., *Darwin to Einstein, Historical Studies on Science and Belief* (London: Longman, 1980).

7   **R. Dawkins,** *River out of Eden* (London: Phoenix, 1995), p. 114.

8   **A. McGrath,** *Dawkins' God* (Oxford: Blackwell, 2005), p. 83.

9   *Science in the National Curriculum* (London: Cassell Education, 1991), p. 21, emphasis mine.

10 A Scheme of Work is jargon for a document used in a school department to outline what the students should be learning. Sometimes these are published as 'off the shelf' schemes. Otherwise, they are written by the department members themselves.

11 Both these titles were published by Heinemann in the 1990s.

12 **R. Dawkins,** *River out of Eden,* p. 114.

13 *Julian of Norwich: A Revelation,* **J. Skinner,** trans. (London: Arthur James, 1996), p. 8.

14 Ibid. p. 8.

15 *Meister Eckhart,* **R. B. Blakney,** trans. (New York: Harper & Bros, 1941).

16 **F. A. Schaeffer,** *True Spirituality* (London: Hodder and Stoughton, 1972), p. 26.

17 **R. Dawkins,** *The Selfish Gene* (Oxford University Press, 1989), p. 198.

18 **A. McGrath,** *Dawkins' God* (Oxford: Blackwell, 2005), p. 85.

19 **C. Jones, G. Wainwright** and **E. Yarnold,** eds., *The Study of Spirituality* (London: SPCK, 1986), p. 3.

20 Ibid. p. 8.

21 Ibid. p. 15.

22 **Augustine,** *Confessions IX.10,* **H. Chadwick** (trans) (Oxford University Press, 1991), p. 162.

23 **Jones et al,** op. cit. p. 15.

24 **Jones et. al.,** p.10.

25 **F. A. Schaeffer,** *Genesis in Space and Time* (London: Hodder and Stoughton, 1973), p. 48.

26 *Meister Eckhart,* **R. B. Blakney,** trans. p. 85.

27 Ibid. p. 85.

28 Ibid. p. 315.

29 **F. A. Schaeffer,** *True Spirituality,* p. 101.

30 Ibid. p. 142.

31 Ibid. p. 141.

32 **F. A. Schaeffer,** *Escape from Reason* (London: Inter-Varsity Press, 1968), pp. 10ff.

33 Ibid. p. 9.

34 Ibid.

35 **Aquinas,** quoted in **K. Armstrong,** *A History of God* (London: Heinemann, 1993), p. 238.

36 **F. A. Schaeffer,** *Escape from Reason,* pp. 10ff.

37 **Aquinas,** quoted in **K. Armstrong,** *A History of God* (London: Heinemann, 1993), p. 239.

38 Ibid. p. 239.

39 C. S. Lewis, *Miracles* (London: Collins, 1947), p. 12.

40 F. J. Tipler, *The Physics of Immortality* (London: Macmillan, 1994), p. 264.

41 Armstrong, *A History of God*, p. 347.

42 Ibid. p. 408.

43 Ibid. p. 410.

44 Ibid. p. 409.

45 Ibid. p. 340.

The new physics

4.1 Religious concepts

Concepts of the New Physics frequently revolve around the Big Bang theory. Popularisers and apologists for the Big Bang theory frequently use language which owes more to the religiosity they claim to despise than to the neutrally scientific. Television astronomer Heather Couper comments thus on the 'nothing' that she believes existed before the Big Bang.

It was a 'nothing' so profound it defies human comprehension.[1]

Alan Guth, developer of the idea of Cosmic Inflation, as an adjunct to the Big Bang theory, puts it in an equally 'religious' manner:

To the average person it might seem obvious that nothing can happen in nothing. But to a quantum physicist, nothing is, in fact, something.[2]

A couple of pages later, he has this amazing comment:

Quantum theory also holds that a vacuum, like atoms, is subject to quantum uncertainties. This means that things can materialise out of the vacuum, although they tend to vanish back into it quickly … *this phenomenon has never been observed directly* … (emphasis mine).[3]

Such comments as these cannot be classed as scientific comments. They are statements of opinion, rather than fact, incapable of scientific test. In other words, they are religious statements.

4.2 The origin of Hawking's ideas

One of the principal problems associated with the New Physics is that it is so incredibly complicated. The whole subject of cosmology, as discussed by Hawking, is a lifetime's work, and quite outside the scope of this book.

Stephen Hawking is the Lucasian Professor of Mathematics at the University of Cambridge. He is well known for his work in theoretical physics, despite the tremendous handicap of motor neurone disease. The essence of Hawking's theories is difficult to grasp, even with the advantage given by the popularization available in *A Brief History of Time*.[4] However, although the nature of time itself is difficult to follow from Hawking's discussions, the development of his thinking in that direction may open a connective path between the development of high scientific thinking and the connected issues.

There are many more detailed criticisms of Hawking's views in particular, and the Big Bang view in general.[5]

To begin to comment on his ideas, Hawking's views on the question of time need to be noted. His first view is that of Einstein's—that it is not possible to understand time without reference to space. Referring to space implies a measurement of distance in three dimensions, or maybe, confusingly, four. Time is therefore another measurement of progress. His second view is Aristotle's—that the natural state of objects was to be at rest. This implies that an object would remain still if no force were applied. If a force were to be applied, the object would begin to move.

Thirdly, we must note the view of Galileo, who first perceived a flaw in Aristotelian physics. An apocryphal tale has it that Galileo dropped weights from the famous Leaning Tower of Pisa in order to prove that different masses landed at the same time. It is unlikely that the story is true, but similar experiments can be carried out today. Newton developed the idea in his Law of Motion. His First Law stated that a body will continue in its present state of rest *or to move at an uniform velocity*, unless acted upon by an external force. The new concept was that of uniform velocity as being a natural state, and this was followed by his Second Law. This states the mathematical relationship:

$$F = m \times a$$
(F is force, m is mass, and a is acceleration)

This allows us to explain Galileo's supposed experiment by stating that the difference in weight (force due to gravity) of the dropped objects is cancelled by the difference in mass, leading us to presume a constant acceleration due to gravity on all the objects. However, the corollary of these laws is that it is difficult to tell the difference between rest and uniform velocity. One can sit in train A at a station, and when train B, on the adjacent track, begins to move, one momentarily believes that it is train A which is moving in a direction opposite to that in which train B is actually moving. The implication is that all movement is therefore relative and that Aristotle's state of rest does not necessarily exist. Similarly, the stationary car is in fact moving rapidly through space as the Earth orbits the Sun at a speed of 30 kilometres per second (which is about 18·5 miles per second).

We note in discussing these matters that one supposed fact, which had not changed from Aristotle to Newton, was the absolute nature of time. However, this, too, was eventually to be called into question when Roemer suggested that light travels at a constant velocity. This is now a recognised fact, but it caused a problem, because Newton had shown that motion was relative—i.e. that if the speed of light was a constant, it must be constant *relative to something else*. When this was first considered, some suggested that space was made of an undetectable substance called ether, through which the light was able to travel. Thus, if the speed of light from an object is measured in the direction of the Earth's motion through the ether, it should differ from its value measured at right angles to this motion. While this is in accord with Newtonian physics, Michelson and Morley showed that both measurements were *exactly the same*—an observation which enabled Einstein to show that time itself is relative and not absolute. Hawking explains it thus:

In Newton's theory, if a pulse of light is sent from one place to another, different observers would agree on the time that the journey took (since time is absolute), but will not agree on how far the light has travelled (since space is not absolute). Since the speed of the light is just the distance it has travelled divided by the time it has taken, different observers would measure different speeds for the light. In relativity, on the other hand, all observers *must* agree on how fast light travels. They still, however, do not agree on the distance the light has travelled, so they must therefore now also disagree over the time it has taken … In other words, the theory of relativity put an end to the idea of absolute time [6]

It is discussion on the nature of time which Hawking took further and which underpins the philosophy of the New Physics.

It follows from this discussion that, because time is relative, like space, rather than absolute, it can be included as a fourth dimension in the classical Euclidean geometry. It has become common, therefore, to refer to *space-time*. Where Euclidean geometry suggested that the three angles of a triangle on a plane surface add up to 180 degrees, such a geometry can now be applied to four dimensions. However, non-Euclidean geometries can now be postulated, where the angles of a triangle do not add up to 180 degrees. For example, in spherical geometry, a triangle drawn with a 90 degree angle to an apex fixed at the pole, and its base line on the equator, will include right-angles at all three corners. While such geometries are impossible to draw, they may be worked mathematically. It follows that if space-time is essentially Euclidean in its dimensionality, the universe must either have existed for an infinite time or else have had an origin at a particular point in time. However, if the space-time continuum is non-Euclidean in its properties, another possibility opens up. As Hawking has it:

It is possible for space-time to be finite in extent and yet to have no singularities that formed a boundary or edge.[7]

We may understand this with reference to a two-dimensional drawing on the surface of the Earth. Such a drawing will appear flat to us, but if we draw a line in either of the two dimensions (longitude and latitude) they will eventually return to where they started. Hawking suggests that space-time *may* be like this. He goes on to propose that this consideration eliminates the need to consider God, stating:

There would be no singularity at which the laws of science broke down and no edge of space-time at which one would have to appeal to God or some new law to set the boundary conditions for space-time…. The universe would be completely self-contained and not affected by anything outside itself. It would neither be created nor destroyed. It would just BE.[8]

Hawking's view of the universe is bleak and determined both causally and finally, as it proposes a universe, which *had* to work out the way it did. What should be noticed, however, is that Hawking's universe is not a neutral construct. It is a universe in which Hawking's concept of God, or rather lack of concept of God, is a fundamental part of the model. It is the opinion of this author that many school physics teachers will only have a vague idea of Hawking's ideas, important as they are to a study of modern cosmology. However, they will assume that his ideas are more or less factual, or, at the very least, objective. This offers an explanation for the teaching of physics in an environment more atheistic than Newton would have liked—indeed, more atheistic than Einstein would have liked. Indeed, if Hawking allows for any kind of god—and some of his comments suggest that he is not entirely atheistic—then his god is an extreme example of Lewis's naturalistic God described in the previous chapter. Hawking says:

Einstein once asked the question: 'How much choice did God have in constructing the universe?'... If the no-boundary proposal is correct, he had no freedom at all to choose initial conditions.[9]

Such is Hawking's reputation that it is easy to forget that we are dealing with the realm of theoretical rather than experimental physics. Hawking's comments about the attributes of God, and even the boundary conditions for space-time, are incapable of experimental investigation. Einstein's ideas of the relative nature of time *are* capable of investigation. It is too often assumed that the views of Hawking and others are a natural corollary of Einstein. The introduction of God into his comments brings a spiritual dimension to Hawking's views, albeit his spirituality is a non-spirituality.

What is frequently overlooked is that, as Hawking himself admits, his theories are themselves based on assumptions. Hawking assumes that:
- Einstein's relativity theory is correct
- The universe has no bounds

Both these assumptions are difficult to understand, but do not depend on each other. The first assumption is eminently reasonable, as it would appear to be supported by the scientific observations. The second assumption, however, requires more analysis. It will be shown that the second assumption exists, not because the evidence demands it, but because Hawking's presuppositions demand it. This means that the second assumption is a faith position, rather than an evidential position.

That this second assumption of Hawking can be challenged is of great importance to the subject of science education. How correctly to teach the so-called Big Bang theory of cosmology is an issue that constantly vexes physics teachers. It is acknowledged by most that Big Bang cosmology is frequently misunderstood and misapplied. Dare we suggest that it is often misunderstood by physics teachers themselves? It is a common misconception that the Big Bang theory teaches that matter once existed in one part of the cosmos, and exploded, expanding to fill the existing vacuum of space. This is not correct. Big Bang cosmologists actually teach that space itself only took up the small space of the original *singularity*, and after the actual Big Bang, it is space itself that expanded. Bill Bryson, in his usual entertaining way, explains it thus:

It is natural but wrong to visualize the singularity as a kind of pregnant dot hanging in a dark, boundless void. But there is no space, no darkness. The singularity has no around around it. There is no space for it to occupy, no place for it to be. We can't even ask how long it has been there—whether it has just lately popped into being, like a good idea, or whether it has been there for ever, quietly awaiting the right moment. Time doesn't exist. There is no past for it to emerge from.[10]

Because this view of the universe is so complex and so detailed, the common misconception is that, however difficult to understand it is, it must be an actual statement of how things really are. There are, however, scientists challenging one or both of Hawking's assumptions, so it is only fair to ask the reasoning behind Hawking's second assumption.

4.3 The Copernican Principle
It is fair to say that Copernicus would probably not have recognised his eponymous principle. The Copernican Principle states that on a large scale (of millions of light-years) the universe is both isotropic and homogeneous. The latter implies that matter is spread out roughly evenly throughout the entire universe. The former implies that the universe looks the same in

whatever direction one looks. The common misconception of the Big Bang theory is that it implies that matter is spreading out through an infinite cosmos. This is not what Big Bang theorists believe. They believe that matter takes up the entire cosmos. As Carl Sagan put it: 'The cosmos is all that is or ever was or ever will be';[11] a statement of unqualified religious belief, if ever I saw one

The question needs to be asked: why do cosmologists construct such a complicated model?

Hubble discovered the effect known as the red-shift. Elements, when heated, give off radiation which is not completely mixed, but which exists in only certain values. This is because electrons are promoted to different energy levels, and the energy given out, as the electrons' excitation energy is dispersed, can only be equal to the drops in energy, as the electrons return to their 'natural' levels. Such spectra are easily recognised, and will be in the form of bands of light at certain frequencies, while other frequencies will be dark. In fact, the actual absorption lines appear dark against a background of the rest of the spectrum—a sort of colourful negative image This concept can be seen in the diagram below.[12]

Starlight shows some of these spectra for elements, but the spectral lines are at frequencies lower than they should be. The entire spectra is said to be 'shifted' towards the red end of the spectrum—hence the term 'red-shift'. This effect is similar to what I used to call the 'nee-naw' effect Old-

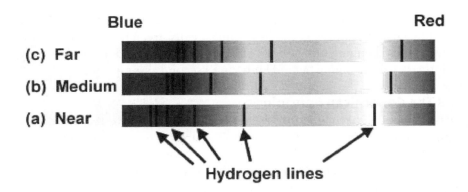

Hydrogen lines

fashioned fire engines would have a 'nee-naw' siren As the fire engine approached the observer on the pavement, the pitch of the siren would increase, but would decrease as the appliance went passed and started to move away from the observer. The latter effect is like red-shift. The former effect would be a 'blue-shift', if observed in stars. However, galaxies usually appear to be red-shifted rather than blue-shifted. In addition, Hubble assumed that the further away objects were, the more they would be red-shifted.[13]

This analogy, it will be pointed out, is not perfect. My 'nee-naw' effect is actually a version of the so-called Doppler Effect, caused by differential velocities. However, the red-shift in galaxies, though possibly containing a slight Doppler component, is thought to be caused mainly by the expansion of space itself rather than motion through it.

The classical Big Bang model suggests that the cosmos is a sort of three-dimensional sphere, expanding through a fourth dimension. Because we cannot visualise such four-dimensional models, we use, as an analogy, the idea of a two-dimensional surface expanding through a third. The analogy used in many school text books is that of a lot of galaxies drawn on the surface of a balloon. As the balloon is inflated, the galaxies on the surface get further from each other. What is often not made clear from these text books is that the space in the middle of the balloon is not really there. The expanding surface is all that there is

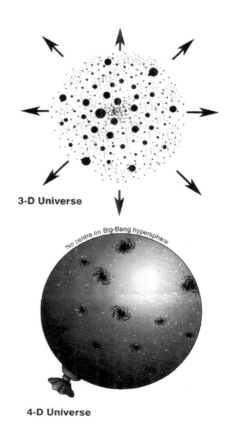

3-D Universe

4-D Universe

of the universe—a three-dimensional expanding surface, expanding through a fourth dimension—which is impossible for us to visualise.[14]

If your head is by now beginning to spin, the question that will be occurring to you is: why is this model so complicated? It is a perfectly fair question to ask. The Big Bangers will tell you that the model has to be that complicated because of Hubble's observations. If that is what they say, they are incorrect. Much simpler models are possible. Hubble himself suggested that the observations could be interpreted differently.

Such a condition [these red shifts] would imply that we occupy a unique position in the universe, ... But the unwelcome supposition of a favored location must be avoided at all costs ... is intolerable ... moreover, it represents a discrepancy with the theory because the theory postulates homogeneity.[15]

Notice the grounds on which Hubble rejects his original suggestion. He cannot accept the idea of the earth being in a favoured position, describing such a view as 'unwelcome' and 'intolerable'. Why is such a view intolerable? He rejects the view because it does not coincide with his views of a secular, godless universe.

George Ellis has co-authored many papers with Stephen Hawking. An interview with Ellis in *Scientific American* went as follows:

'People need to be aware that there is a range of models that could explain the observations,' Ellis argues. 'For instance, I can construct you a spherically symmetrical universe with Earth at its center, and you cannot disprove it based on observations.' Ellis has published a paper on this. 'You can only exclude it on philosophical grounds. In my view there is absolutely nothing wrong in that. What I want to bring into the open is the fact that we are using philosophical criteria in choosing our models. A lot of cosmology tries to hide that.'[16],[17]

The diagram[18] shows the 3D misconception, which nevertheless explains the observations, and a 4D balloon model. The 4D model was invented simply as a means of saying that there is nothing special about the earth or its inhabitants.

The point that we need to underline is that the Copernican Principle—

Hawking's second assumption—is not necessarily correct. It is an assumption, on which the entire cosmology stands and falls. Humphreys' cosmology, for example, stands on the basis that Hawking's second assumption is wrong. Hawking's second assumption is based only on the philosophical need to develop a model of cosmic evolution which does not include God. The most unusual characteristics of the model—that the universe has no boundary and hence no centre—are not required by the scientific observations. They are required only because of the philosophical position of the scientists concerned.

Hawking reports:

Einstein once asked the question: 'How much choice did God have in constructing the universe?' … If the no-boundary proposal is correct, he had no freedom at all to choose initial conditions.[19]

However, Hawking's entire construct is mathematical. We might say that it has started from the lower storey and has ended up in the lower storey and provides no hope or promise of fulfilment. This critique, in contrast, is rooted in the Christian concept of *eschato*; the idea that the cosmos has a source and a destiny. The fact is that science is not expected to consider words such as hope and this shows how complete the eradication of the upper storey of the Christian, Platonic and Aristotelian conceptualisation of the universe seems to have been. The train of thought that Aquinas put in place seems to have led to a divorce between the upper and lower storeys.

4.4 The Anthropic Cosmological Principle

While the above commentary on the views of Hawking seems to be a complete chapter in its own terms, we must, however, note that, despite being the most popular, Hawking's cosmological theories are by no means the only ones in the market place, even in non-creationist, secular circles. An alternative view of the universe and its development has been propounded by Barrow and Tipler—namely the so-called *Anthropic Cosmological Principle*.[20] As a generalisation, it can be suggested that scientific thinking, since Aristotle, has gradually moved humanity away from the centre of the universe. What is so startling about this 'Anthropic

Principle' is that humanity is placed right back at the centre of everything. The perhaps dominant high theory of science seems to preclude the questions of morality and spirituality, which lie at the core, however inadequately expressed, in traditional curricular thinking. Such questions are to be found (perhaps as relics) in a wholly inadequate form in the formulation of the National Curriculum. The Anthropic Principle does appear to offer science education the opportunity of returning the principles of morality, hope, meaning and personal engagement to the core of the curriculum. The tyranny of a mechanistic prescription, which educators will recognise as the death of the imagination—which alone gives life to their profession—may thus become less likely.

The Anthropic Cosmological Principle is by no means a fellow traveller of creationism. The concepts developed by Barrow and Tipler accept the concept of cosmological evolution. John D Barrow is Research Professor of Mathematical Sciences at the University of Cambridge, while Frank Tipler is a professor of Mathematical Physics at Tulane University, New Orleans. Their view is that all events are *random*—they merely indicate that they believe not every event to be equally *likely*. In effect, the process has been not unlike playing a board game with a biased die. One could then see which events were more or less likely, in retrospect, by examining those events which have, in fact, taken place. They surmise that the universe has evolved in such a way as to make life, and eventually human life, possible here on earth. They believe that the present state of the universe implies that it was always more likely that the universe would turn out the way it has done The die must have been loaded in favour of people evolving. They infer that it follows that the whole evolution of the universe leads inevitably to the evolution of man. For this reason, their cosmology is no more in tune with biblical truth than that of Hawking.

Barrow and Tipler suggest that there are two essential versions of the Anthropic Principle. These are the Weak and the Strong Anthropic Principles.

The Weak Anthropic Principle may be stated thus:

The observed values of all physical and cosmological quantities are not equally probable but they take on values restricted by the requirement that there exist sites where carbon-based life can evolve and by the requirement that the Universe be old enough for it to have already done so.[21]

This, the claim, is close to the explanation already given; that is, a biasing of the die.

The Weak Anthropic Principle tries to tie a precise statement to the notion that any cosmological observations made by astronomers are biased by an all-embracing selection effect: our own existence.[22]

Where classical scientific observation purports to be performed by a neutral observer (i.e. one who is not connected with the experiment), the Weak Anthropic Principle recognises that such neutrality of perspective is never possible, as the existence of the observer affects the experiment. This is a principle that has, of course, long been recognised in the social, if not natural, sciences.

Barrow and Tipler define the Strong Anthropic Principle thus:

The Universe must have those properties which allow life to develop within it at some stage in its history.[23]

The Strong Anthropic Principle thus leads inevitably to the process of life and human life—a kind of secular predestination. In a similar way, Kosko, a modern philosopher of science, has observed that 'the Universe is as it is so that we would be here'.[24]

The problem with the Strong Anthropic Principle would seem to be that it is so convenient. The universe is the way it is because that is inevitably how it would turn out. Yet Barrow and Tipler would strongly deny any sense that their argument implies intelligent design. Kosko's problem with the Strong Anthropic Principle is that 'the Anthropic principle opens a Pandora's box of smart worlds when it tries to explain just one'. If the universe is as it is, because it is inevitable that it would turn out the way it is, it is surely not inappropriate for the scientist to ask 'why?' Kosko continues.

It still does not explain why just asking a question or having a brain or brain-like thing picks out a world line. It gives no mechanism for how it picks or prunes a world line. We might as well say the universe is here because this rock or star is here and it would not be here if the universe did not unfold to make it so.[25]

Biblical creationists, or proponents of intelligent design, would welcome the theory's implication of a sense of purpose. With reference to our subject matter, it may or may not be relevant to include reference to the Anthropic Cosmological Principle to school students learning physics, but they should not be shielded from knowing that a good many scientists—and not just Christians—see the universe in terms of purpose and design. Science has long been seen as purposelessly pursuing a theory which demonstrates purposelessness. Whatever we do not yet know about nature as a whole, we do know that humanity cannot continue in that direction and remain humane. Nicolson captures something of this perspective when he says:

The difference between 'old' and 'new' is shown in the difference between generations who felt their earth was the centre of the universe and generations who learned that their earth is no such thing. Yet, though we have paid lip service to that theory, we have felt our convictions fall before poet after poet, who, knowing with his intellect the hypothesis of Copernicus, still felt the 'little world of man' remains a solid ball beneath his feet, the centre of his universe.[26]

It is interesting that Tipler is even prepared to take this Anthropic Principle even further by postulating a type of God who transcends the universe. It is his contention that all events in space-time can be extrapolated to the so-called 'Omega Point', and it is this 'Omega Point', which 'takes the place of God'. Again, his theorisation is backed up by a considerable mathematical infrastructure. He says,

A given universe exists necessarily if it contains observers all the way into the Omega Point. The collective observations (and actions) of all observers bring the entire universe into existence; equivalently, the past, present and future exist because these regions of space-time are observed by the Omega Point.

This formulation is, of course, reminiscent of the eighteenth-century British philosopher George Berkeley's idea that the universe's existence is due to the fact that it is under continual observation by God. The sceptical observer might comment that the dependence of the theory on observation 'all the way into the Omega Point' is a rejuvenation of the medieval angelology

4.5 Conclusion

Scientific progress, at least in Physics, has become complex. It will be noted, however, that the universes of Hawking on the one hand, and of Barrow and Tipler on the other, are not places capable of experimental investigation. They are philosophical constructs, based on assumptions that are necessary to an atheistic cosmology—assumptions which can fairly be challenged by creation scientists. If Hawking's ideas removed the upper storey from Aristotle's universe, then Barrow and Tipler have reinstated it, in such away that it is inextricably linked with the lower storey by procession.

The argument we have been expounding is twofold. First, we have seen that there is an inextricable link between science and its spiritual context. Historically, this link has been apparent, but it is also elucidated in more modern writing. Secondly, this spiritual context of science, if it is always present, should therefore be present in the science education of children. It seems appropriate to analyse how far teachers are aware of this 'hidden education' in their lessons and how we may put it to use in the further understanding of what pupils actually learn during their lessons.

Notes

1 **H. Couper** and **N. Henbest,** *Big Bang* (London: Dorling Kindersley Publishing, 1997), p. 8.

2 **B. Lemley,** *Guth's Grand Guess*, **Discover** vol. 23, April 2002, p. 35.

3 Ibid. p. 38.

4 **S.W. Hawking,** *A Brief History of Time* (New York: Transworld, 1998).

5 A recommended work on the subject would be: **A. Williams** and **J. Hartnett,** *Dismantling the Big Bang* (Green Forest, AR: Master Books, 2005).

6 Ibid. p. 135.

7 Ibid.

8 Ibid. p. 136.

9 Ibid. p. 174.

10 Bill Bryson, *A Short History of Nearly Everything* (London: Black Swan, 2003), p. 28.

11 C. Sagan, *Cosmos* (London: Abacus, 1995), p. 4.

12 Diagram taken from **R. Humphreys,** *Our galaxy is the centre of the universe, 'quantized' red shifts show,* TJ **16**(2): 95–104, August 2002.

13 Some more recent evidence casts doubt on aspects of this observation. Readers are referred to **A. Williams** and **J. Hartnett,** *Dismantling the Big Bang* (Green Forest, AR: Master Books: 2005).

14 See **R. Humphreys,** *Starlight and Time* (Green Forest, AR: Master Books: 2003), p. 14.

15 E. Hubble, *The Observational Approach to Cosmology* (Oxford: Clarendon, 1937).

16 W. Wayt Gibbs, 1995. Profile: George F. R. Ellis; Thinking Globally, Acting Universally, *Scientific American* 273(4): 28–29.

17 It should be noted that Answers in Genesis do not take a geocentric view—the view that the earth is the centre of the universe. There is much evidence, however, to suggest that our galaxy is near to the centre. See **J. Hartnett,** *A creationist cosmology in a galactocentric universe*, TJ **19**(1), 73–81.

18 Taken from **Hartnett,** op. cit., reference 17.

19 S.W. Hawking, op. cit., p. 174.

20 J.D. Barrow and **F.J. Tipler,** *The Anthropic Cosmological Principle* (Oxford: Clarendon Press, 1986).

21 Ibid, p. 16.

22 Ibid, p. 15.

23 Ibid, p. 21.

24 B. Kosko, *Fuzzy Thinking, the New Science of Fuzzy Logic* (New York: Hyperion, 1993), p. 270.

25 Ibid. 271–272

26 M. Nicolson, *Science and Imagination* (Ithaca, NY: Cornell University Press, 1956), p. 1.

Classroom practice— the context of the inquiry

Introduction

With all the paperwork and administration inherent in today's education system, it would be understandable if few teachers wished to spend time in a consideration of science in a spiritual context. Stated baldly, the teacher might suppose that this is a new addition to the teaching load, already groaning under the strain of content and assessment. However, it is the contention of this author that science is inextricably linked with its spiritual context. A consideration of the implications of this fact in the classroom situation is essential in order to improve our teaching of science and to help pupils better understand it. The teaching of science imparts spiritual values, whether the teacher realises this or not.

The purpose of this chapter is to outline the thinking behind the questionnaire, which formed the basis for the studies in the following two chapters.

The explanation of science

In science, as in other subjects of the curriculum, the teacher has first to engage the pupils by capturing their imagination. Most pupils find it fascinating to visit museums. Dinosaurs and other extinct beasts make particularly exciting exhibits for younger students. Meticulous detail is taken in presentation, especially regarding how the information is delivered to the observer. Today's museum-goers are unlikely to want to spend time reading from dreary typewritten notes. Bright boards with bold lettering, audio commentary or video links—the signs of a visual age—ensure that a story is told, and the observer is brought into it.

The illustration below is taken from the BBC's website—a revision guide for GCSE students.[1] (The abbreviations GCSE stand for General

Certificate of Secondary Education. GCSEs are the principal matriculation examinations in the education systems of England, Wales and Northern Ireland, and are usually taken by students at the age of sixteen.) On the web page itself, horse evolution is described as a good example of evolution, thus:

One of the few animals for which we have a fairly complete evolutionary record is the horse, as all the main stages of horse evolution have been preserved in *fossil* form. Over 60 million years the horse evolved from a dog-sized rainforest-dwelling creature, into an animal adapted to plains-dwelling and standing up to 2 metres high.[2]

Two details are of particular interest. Firstly, there is a correlation implied between the progression of age and size, so that the horses get gradually bigger, from the *Eohippus* (or 'Dawn Horse') to Przewalski's Horse (a modern-day wild horse). Secondly, the diagram shows a gradual development of the hoof from an extended middle toe on the foot of the *Eohippus*. Such illustrations tell a good story and make good displays in museums, encyclopaedias and text books. However, the illustration bears little relationship even to modern evolutionary thinking. It is an example of the evolutionary scientists' spiritual (or anti-spiritual) values being presented to the pupil as if they were evidence, when the actual evidence is different.

Closer analysis reveals a considerable number of flaws in the story of horse evolution. The gradual increase in size is erroneous. True horses today range in size from the 43 cm Fallabella to the Clydesdale, standing at over 2 metres. Secondly, the toe development is erroneous. There are horses today which have three toes, as reported by O.C. Marsh.[3] Thirdly, this neat sequence of horse fossils is not found in one place anywhere in the world. On the contrary, the fossils are gathered together from different sites and arranged in this order *because* of the theory that they are supposed to have evolved from each other, not as proof that they did so. To use the diagram as evidence for evolution is therefore circular reasoning.

Moreover, the very use of the word 'Eohippus' on the diagram is indicative of presuppositional influence. In palaeontology, it is understood that the discoverer of a fossil has the right to name it. The so-called 'Eohippus' fossil was discovered in 1841 by Richard Owen.[4] He named the fossil *Hyracotherium*. It follows that the BBC website should have used this name. Owen named the fossil thus because he saw that it was similar to a hyrax. He saw no connection between his discovery and horses. The connection is an invention of the evolutionists. The diagram is so erroneous that it is an embarrassment even to evolutionists. Heribert-Nilsson has said that 'the family tree of the horse is beautiful and continuous only in the textbooks',[5] while Eldridge has described a museum exhibition showing the same sequence of horse evolution as 'lamentable'.[6] The actual use of the term 'Dawn Horse', and the very juxtaposition of the so-called horse ancestors, is simply a statement of belief. The BBC website's claim that there exists a 'fairly complete evolutionary record … (of) the horse' is false. The claim, together with the use of the diagram, makes a statement of the religious or spiritual values of the article writer, and contributes nothing towards the students' understanding of science.

It would seem that the need to 'tell a good story' has led those creating such displays to bend their judgement and to present data which is tendentious rather than scientific. It is notable that such representations are particularly likely to be presented to students of school age in the apparent service of simplicity. After all, a good science teacher is a populariser of science, because it is desirable that information imparted to pupils is memorable and it is more likely to be memorable if it is attractive and succinct.

Lewontin has an explanation for this sort of dogmatism.

As evolutionary theory has developed over the last one hundred years and become technologically and scientifically sophisticated, as vague notions of inheritance have become converted into a very precise theory of the structure and function of DNA, so the evolutionary view of human nature has developed into a modern, scientific-sounding apparatus that makes it seem every bit as unchallengeable as the theories of divine providence in an earlier age.[7]

This is a characteristically honest comment from this atheist evolutionary geneticist, who once said:

We take the side of science *in spite* of the patent absurdity of some of its constructs, *in spite* of its failure to fulfil many of its extravagant promises of health and life, *in spite* of the tolerance of the scientific community for unsubstantiated just-so stories, because we have a prior commitment, a commitment to materialism. It is not that the methods and institutions of science somehow compel us to accept a material explanation of the phenomenal world, but, on the contrary, that we are forced by our *a priori* adherence to material causes to create an apparatus of investigation and a set of concepts that produce material explanations, no matter how counter-intuitive, no matter how mystifying to the uninitiated. Moreover, that materialism is an absolute, for we cannot allow a Divine Foot in the door[8] (emphasis in original).

Lewontin seems to suggest that such scientific views, as illustrated in his first quote, are an artefact of the society in which we live. They represent the bias of the image-packager and have an ideological function. While they represent an 'effective communication', this is achieved at the cost of the truth principle. A similar scenario affects broader areas of the media-packaging of scientific educational material. In this context, for example, the views of Richard Dawkins, and other successful popularisers of science, are highly individualistic. For example, after describing how a digger wasp lays her eggs inside a caterpillar, paralysing but not killing the caterpillar, so that her larvae can feed on fresh meat, he says:

This sounds savagely cruel, but … Nature is not cruel, only pitilessly indifferent. This is one of the hardest lessons for humans to learn. We cannot admit that things might be neither good nor evil, neither cruel nor kind, but simply callous—indifferent to all suffering, lacking all purpose.[9]

Lewontin seems to oppose this view, commenting on its implications thus:

We are, in Richard Dawkin's metaphor, lumbering robots created by our DNA, body and mind. But the view that we are totally at the mercy of internal forces present within ourselves from birth is part of a deep ideological commitment that goes under the name of *reductionism* … This individualistic view of the biological world is simply a reflection of the ideologies of the bourgeois revolutions of the eighteenth century that placed the individual at the centre of everything.[10]

In effect, we may derive from this the further observation that Dawkins and his emulators are, in fact, purveyors of a somewhat edited view of reality. Their views are, of course, not a theology, as they are explicitly atheistic. They may, however, qualify as a sort of anti-theology. They may or may not be innocuous, but they are certainly tendentious. It is interesting to note that these views, and the associated views on religious teaching in schools, are likely to be cited in favour of the views of the scientific curriculum, which would most emphatically deny a place for the spiritual within it—at least in any traditional sense of the word.

Science education, scientific approaches

The premise adopted, for the purposes of this study, is that *values* (including spiritual ones) are inherent in every aspect of science and that the implication of this understanding for the classroom teacher is that they must teach science in a way which conveys values (moral, social and spiritual) to the pupils. However, the question must be asked as to the extent to which science teachers agree with this reasoning and how much they are aware of the values actually being propagated. These questions are such that they should lead to an explicit enquiry into teachers' views on these matters and the need to discuss the appropriate method for collecting such information.

At this point, a question arises as to whether the enquiry should follow a qualitative or a quantitative research model. Quantitative research is at once appealing and satisfying to the scientific mind. It has the feel of experimental results by means of numerical data. Graphs can be drawn and statistical correlations can be calculated.

For example, imagine an investigation in which students measure the stability of plastic bottles in which different amounts of water are placed. An empty pop bottle is placed on a board and a measured amount of water is introduced. The board is slowly lifted from one end until the bottle just topples over. The angle between board and table is then measured. A large number of figures for volume of water and angle of toppling can be generated. Graphs can then be plotted and conclusions drawn. The investigation described enables pupils to understand that the position of the centre of gravity of a structure, in relation to its base and height, affects the stability of the structure. While this could be observed qualitatively, the above investigation can locate the position of the centre of gravity in a structure of optimum stability. The graph plotted, of angle of toppling vs. water volume, produces an inverse parabola. The student can be shown that the optimum position for the centre of gravity is represented by the maximum point of the curve. This enables an accurate calculation of the point required, even if the student has not hit on the correct measurement by chance. The shape of the curve produced also allows conclusions about the behaviour of the system to be drawn. The difference between a qualitative and a quantitative analysis of the above system can be aptly illustrated by the typical pupils' responses—'The second structure is *more* stable than the first' and 'the second structure is *twice as* stable as the first'. The second response is deemed to be 'more scientific' than the first.

Such procedures, and this is only an example, may be used to justify research which produces a numeric outcome seeming to have a particular attraction for a science teacher. Slightly more sociological would be a questionnaire asking teachers their opinions on a number of topics. Answers could be gathered and analysed statistically. The problem with such research is that it requires a very large sample to be statistically valid. Wilson points out that:

The causes of social phenomena are usually multiple ones and an experiment to study them requires large numbers of people often for lengthy periods. This requirement limits the usefulness of the experimental method.[11]

There are two main reasons why quantitative analysis was not used for the present inquiry. The first of these was purely pragmatic. It was felt that it would be unlikely to be possible to obtain sufficient responses to questionnaires on the subject of science and spirituality to generate valid statistics, without a greater outlay of time and resources than was available. The author has felt that both the availability of access and time to be insufficient.

The second reason, perhaps more pertinent, concerns the nature of information required. What is required for the survey is the attitude of teachers to their own teaching and to notions of spirituality and science.

Questions which generate statistics need to have closed responses. For example:

Q. Do you agree with the statement that …?

A. Yes ❑   No ❑

Or

Q What is your age range?

A 0–12   ❑

  13–20   ❑

  21–35   ❑

  36–65   ❑

  66 or over ❑

These sorts of questions are not conducive to elucidating opinions. A question, such as 'What is your response to this statement …?' will not yield neatly categorisable answers. Yet this would appear to be the sort of questioning required for this inquiry. Judith Bell says, 'Researchers adopting a qualitative perspective are more concerned to understand individuals' perceptions of the world. They seek insight rather than statistical analysis.'[12] For these two reasons—practical and pragmatic—it has been decided to use qualitative rather than quantitative research methods.

The present study is interested in how religious beliefs (or lack of them) affect the approach of the teacher to the teaching of scientific topics. This will involve situation coding. Phrases which reveal something of the subjects' opinions will need to be analysed to determine the background to the answers. The answers can then be interpreted in the light of the perceived religious views of the subject. These views are usually not directly stated but can be inferred from the answers given.

The next chapter looks at the justification for each of the questions and a rationale of the expected responses.

Notes

1 BBC Bitesize Revision guide: Biology: Variation and Inheritance: Examples of Evolution 2: http://www.bbc.co.uk/schools/gcsebitesize/biology/variationandinheritance/3evolutionrev6.shtml.

2 Ibid.

3 **O. C. Marsh,** 'Recent polydactyl horses', *American Journal of Science 43*, 1892, pp. 339–354—as quoted in *Creation Research Society Quarterly* correspondence, Vol. 30, December 1993, p. 125.

4 Owen was a renowned and brilliant anatomist. In the same year (1841) he coined the word 'dinosaur'. Later on he was vocal in his rejection of Darwin's ideas.

5 **Nils Heribert-Nilsson,** *Synthetische Artbildung* (Gleerup, Sweden: Lund University, 1954); cited in **Luther Sunderland,** *Darwin's Enigma: Fossils and Other Problems*, 4th Ed. (Santee, CA: Master Books, 1988), p. 81.

6 **Niles Eldredge,** quoted by **Sunderland,** op. cit., p. 78.

7 **R.C. Lewontin,** *The Doctrine of DNA, Biology as Ideology* (Penguin, 1991), p. 89.

8 **R.C. Lewontin,** 'Billions and billions of demons', *The New York Review*, p. 31, 9 January 1997.

9 **R. Dawkins,** *River out of Eden* (Pheonix, 1995), p. 112.

10 **R.C. Lewontin** (1991) p. 107.

11 **N.J. Wilson** (1979) 'The ethnographic style of research' in *Research Methods in education and the Social Sciences* (Milton Keynes: Open University Educational Enterprises), p. 22.

12 **J. Bell,** *Doing your research project* (Open University Press, 1993), p. 6.

Classroom practice—a survey

The survey was intended to be for science teachers. It was sent only to science teachers. The survey was intended to find out science teachers' attitudes towards spirituality, as mentioned in *Science in the National Curriculum*. The questionnaire is reproduced at the end of this chapter.

The justification for each question is given below, including thoughts on why the question was posed and what sort of answers were expected.

Questionnaires were prepared and sent out in January 1998, with a covering letter explaining the project, to a number of former colleagues of the author, in comprehensive schools in South Wales and Manchester. Of the forty questionnaires sent, twelve were returned. The responses were collated on a question by question basis and were summarised and synthesised. It should be re-emphasised that, where quantities are quoted in this chapter, they are for convenience only and do not have statistical validity. No conclusions can be drawn from the number of responses given with a particular answer.

Contexting questions

Q1 DO YOU HAVE A RELIGIOUS BELIEF?

It has been illustrated above that science education is thought to be free from value judgements, whereas in fact it is full of them. It can be assumed by some, therefore, that science teachers do not need a religious belief, or, if they have one, then it should not impinge upon or interfere with their teaching in any way.

In fact many of my former teaching colleagues have had a religious belief. This has often been a Christian belief, in the broadest possible definition. At one school, a colleague of mine was a practising Muslim. He was science trained, but was also a language-support teacher, and his skills were invaluable in a school with a large proportion of pupils from a Bangladeshi background. We team-taught many classes together and he was well aware of my position as an evangelical Christian. Perhaps it may surprise some that there was a considerable amount of mutual respect between us, and the teamwork, at least from my point of view, was very comfortable.

The question posed here was intended to provide a context for the further comments that the respondent was to make. Answers to subsequent questions might be better understood if it was known whether the respondent had a religious belief or not. It was not the intention to do a statistical analysis. Any calculated figures on how many respondents had a religious belief would be statistically invalid, because the sample size would not have been big enough, and because the questionnaires were sent only to schools where it was reasonably certain that responses would be forthcoming. Nevertheless, it was hoped that this question would give some insight into the way that the other questions were answered.

Exactly half the respondents claimed to have a religious belief, while half did not. This illustrates the point above—it would be absurd to claim that 50% of all science teachers have a religious belief. It could, after all, be argued that those with a religious belief are more likely to respond to such a questionnaire than those that do not. Further study might find, therefore, that the percentage of science teachers with a religious belief is significantly less than 50%. Such numerical analysis was not the purpose of this question.

Q2 DO YOU THINK THERE IS ANY CONNECTION BETWEEN SCIENCE AND RELIGION?

It is Dawkins and others who have suggested that the answer to this question should be 'No'. It is also clear that for many teachers the answer could be 'Yes'.

The question is of a different type to question 1. It is possible that someone with a religious belief might, even so, consider that science and religion are not linked. Such a person has a personal religious belief, but sees this as subjective. They see science as being objective and assume no connection between the two. Such a person is like C. S. Lewis's naturalist. He is described as being different from a supernaturalist, but not necessarily by a belief in God.

Naturalism, without ceasing to be itself, could admit a certain kind of God. The great interlocking event called Nature might be such as to produce at some stage a great cosmic consciousness; an indwelling 'God' arising from the whole process as human mind arises (according to the Naturalists) from human organisms. A Naturalist would not object to that sort of God. The reason is this. Such a God would not stand outside Nature or the total system, would not be existing 'on his own'.[1]

A God of the sort popular Christian writer and apologist, C. S. Lewis describes above could be accommodated, without a teacher having to let such a belief interfere with science. It can also be said that one could believe in a supernatural God, but one who is removed from direct influence—i.e. a God who is confined to Aquinas's Upper Storey, as shown by Schaeffer.[2] Indeed, Schaeffer has gone on to show that this sort of thinking does not necessarily do without God—it simply means that he doesn't matter. He adapts the two-storey model described earlier, as shown below.

Grace

Nature

In response to this question, eight respondents thought that there was a connection between science and religion, while four thought there was not. Of those who thought there was a connection, four had responded 'yes' to the first question and four had responded 'no'. Two had responded to questions 1 and 2 with a double negative, while two respondents had a religious belief, but saw no connection between science and religion.

This mixture of responses was surprising. A double yes or double no response to questions one and would have a certain logic. Those who have a religious belief might be expected to see a connection between science and religion. Those who see no connection between science and religion might be expected to have no religious belief. The most surprising result was those respondents who had a religious belief and yet still felt that there was no connection between science and religion.[3]

Chapter 6

Q3 A PREVIOUS VERSION OF THE NATIONAL CURRICULUM (1990) STATES THAT PUPILS 'SHOULD BE TAUGHT THE MORAL, SOCIAL AND SPIRITUAL IMPLICATIONS OF SCIENCE.' WHAT DO YOU SUPPOSE THE WRITERS OF THE NATIONAL CURRICULUM MEANT BY THE WORD 'SPIRITUAL' IN THE CONTEXT OF SCIENCE?
Much of chapter 3 was concerned with a discussion of the meaning of 'spiritual' in a scientific context. However, many, if not most, science teachers will not have given a great deal of time to a consideration of this matter, except perhaps in the broadest possible terms. The purpose of this extended-answer question was to ascertain the respondent's personal view of what the word 'spiritual' means. This will be coloured, as implied in the question, by what they believe the DfEE (now the DfES) means by the word.[4]

It might reasonably be expected that the answers to this question would be influenced by the respondents' answers to questions 1 and 2. Some of the respondents, who answered 'yes' to both questions, or 'no' to both questions, will be analysed first.

Teachers Arthur and Brenda[5] both responded 'yes' to both questions 1 and 2. Arthur suggested that the writers of the National Curriculum had in mind a 'realisation that science should be used to benefit the development of mankind. [A] search for 'truth', unity.' Brenda said: 'I think that this means the inward beliefs and emotions of individuals.' Both these respondents, who were typical, have focused on humanity rather than on God. The idea of spirituality to them comes from the inside outwards, rather than from above. If we refer to Schaeffer's analyses of Thomist thought, described earlier, these thoughts about spirituality are 'lower storey' ideas. They differ only in that Arthur has generalised over the development of all mankind, whereas Brenda has concentrated on the individual's beliefs. Arthur's comment could perhaps pertain to the 'upper storey' insofar as it appears to put science in the 'upper storey'—i.e. it is science which now benefits mankind rather than God.

These views are not dissimilar from those of the double negative respondents. For example, Colin says: 'I am not convinced it is a religious slant but more connected to personal feelings and interpretations of the curriculum.' In the same way as Arthur and Brenda, Colin has taken a 'lower storey' position, though this might be expected. The emphasis is on what the individual thinks and feels, rather than any connection to God.

Deborah responded 'yes' to question 1 and 'no' to question 2. In the present study, however, Deborah is the first teacher to suggest something approaching an 'upper storey' response. She suggests that the writers of the National Curriculum saw 'spirituality' as 'Creative aspects? Beauty on over-arching order?' The suggestion of order may be intended to come from outside the individual, rather than inside feelings. This is backed up by Deborah's answer to question 6b, where she agrees with Schaeffer's analysis of the universe.

Teachers Eric and Fiona were amongst those who responded 'no' to question 1, but 'yes' to question 2. Eric concentrates on scientific issues on which there can be discussion or debate. He says that the word 'spiritual' could be 'perhaps how people with religious belief could be considered or counselled with regard to issues such as gene testing for disease, abortion or blood transfusion'. This answer suggests confusion, in the minds of teachers, between spiritual and social or moral consequences of science. Fiona, in contrast, takes the question at face value, looking not at what she believes the word 'spiritual' means, but at what she believes the writers of the National Curriculum meant. Fiona says, 'Is it really possible to know the mind of the creators of the National Curriculum? My own interpretation would be they mean a holistic approach to science—how it relates to being "human" in a broader sense.' Once again, a respondent is turning inwards to the individual and his/her response to science rather than starting from God. This, however, is less surprising from a respondent like Fiona, who claims no religious faith, than from Arthur and Brenda, who do.

Q4 DO YOU BELIEVE IT IS RIGHT FOR SPIRITUAL VALUES TO BE TAUGHT IN SCIENCE?

The simple yes/no response to this question will depend on the respondent's answer to question 3.

Five respondents felt that it was right for spiritual values to be taught in science; the rest did not. All those who had responded positively to the first two questions were in this category. It would appear that a religious belief, coupled with the belief that there is a connection between science and religion, leads to the view that spiritual values can be taught in science. Eric was the other respondent in this category.

Q5 DO YOUR OWN BELIEFS EVER INFLUENCE THE WAY YOU APPROACH A TOPIC WITH A CLASS? PLEASE GIVE AN EXAMPLE, HYPOTHETICAL OR OTHERWISE.

It is the contention of chapter 3 that one's spirituality will certainly influence one's actions. This will be especially true in the way that one approaches teaching certain science topics. It was interesting to observe whether teachers agreed with this assertion. It was hoped to be possible to note, from their answers, whether a negative answer to this question is negated or supported by what answers they gave to other questions.

> Suspect any teacher who claims to go into the classroom neutral about such (religious) matters. He is either deceiving himself, or attempting to deceive the children, or both. The claim to be a detached, impartial observer of life will not stand up. Even in a school environment we are actually embroiled in the business of living, and our values and commitments will show in the way we set about it—the way we treat one another and our pupils, the way we talk, the things we do, the situations which call forth our anger or our delight, and the ways we express those reactions.[6]

Christian educationalist Mark Roques believes that avoidance of indoctrination can only be achieved by the teacher honestly facing up to the values that he/she has. His assumption is that indoctrination is *more* likely if the teacher pretends not to have any bias. He says, 'The attempt to conceal or disguise them (our values) may be misleading and unhelpful to children.'[7]

Answers to the first part of question 5 are again split 50–50. However, the great majority of the 'no's' qualified their answer, by inserting a comment, such as 'I hope' or 'not intentionally'. It seems, then, that most teachers accept that their views can be communicated, deliberately or otherwise, to the pupils.

Some teachers gave examples. Arthur suggested the 'big bang theory or oscillating universe, link to creation. Similarity with ideas of creation with other faiths.' Brenda mentioned 'the tactful delivery of a lesson about Galileo's theories'. These two examples are pertinent to sections of syllabuses on astronomy. The importance of these ideas is difficult to grasp without a clear understanding of the ideas and values behind their work. Colin adds: 'Evolution of species—I believe I would adopt a very different approach if I held a religious belief.'

Responsive statements

Q6 THE FOLLOWING STATEMENTS INDICATE A VARIETY OF VIEWS ON THE RELATIONSHIP BETWEEN SCIENCE AND SPIRITUALITY. AS YOU READ THEM, YOU MAY FIND YOURSELF IN AGREEMENT OR DISAGREEMENT WITH THEM. PLEASE COULD YOU STATE WHETHER YOU AGREE OR DISAGREE WITH THEM, GIVING A BRIEF REASON FOR YOUR ANSWER.

a 'The universe we observe has precisely the properties we should expect if there is, at the bottom, no design, no purpose, no evil and no good, nothing but blind pitiless indifference ... DNA neither cares nor knows. DNA just is. And we dance to its music.' (Richard Dawkins)[8]

The thesis of much of Dawkins's work has been the irrationality of DNA. This matter has been discussed above. Dawkins is such a well-known figure in the popularisation of science that it is possible that some teachers will be influenced by his views, even if only by reputation. This bald statement is deliberately provocative, on Dawkins's part. He uses such purposefully extreme statements to shake his readers into taking notice of his opinions.

b 'The universe has order. It is not a chaos. One is able to proceed from the particulars of being to some understanding of its unity. One is able to move ever deeper into the universe and yet never come upon a precipice of incoherence.' (Francis Schaeffer, Christian philosopher)[9]

Schaeffer probably holds a similarly exalted position among evangelical Christian thinkers as Dawkins does among atheistic scientists. His work was an attempt to popularise philosophical thought among an evangelical constituency which was previously resistant to such thinking. It would be fair to say, however, that his views would probably not be widely known among the science teachers who took part in this research. Schaeffer's contention, along with other Christian thinkers, is that the universe itself is testimony to the existence and nature of God. This is indeed the attitude of the Bible, which says, 'The heavens declare the glory of God; And the firmament shows His handiwork.' (Psalm 19:1). Schaeffer's argument is fourfold. First, there is the fact that the universe is there. 'Something is there

rather than nothing being there.'[10] Second, in the comment quoted in the
questionnaire, he is arguing that the order rather than chaos that one sees in
the universe points towards a creator. Third, that this orderliness reveals to
us something of God's character. Fourth, that our own existence points to
God being a person, rather than being some sort of impersonal 'force'. This
is because, argues Schaeffer, a person can only be derived from a person.

If God had stopped his creation with the machine or the plant or the animal, there
would have been no such testimony. But by making man in his own image, the triune
God who communicates ... has created something that reflects his personality.[11]

This idea of the universe witnessing to the existence of a personal God is in
contrast to the ideas of Dawkins. Schaeffer once posed the question:

If the intrinsically personal origin of the universe is rejected, what alternative outlook
can anyone have? ... Man is a product of the impersonal, plus time, plus chance. No
one has ever succeeded in finding personality on this basis.[12]

This is in contrast to Dawkins, who says:

I am against religion because it teaches us to be satisfied with not understanding the
world.[13]

c 'One could still imagine that God created the universe at the instant of the big bang ...
but it would be meaningless to suppose that it was created before the big bang. An
expanding universe does not preclude a creator, but it does place limits on when he
might have carried out his job!' (Stephen Hawking)[14]

In Hawking's famous, popular-style work, *A Brief History of Time*, he is
quite scathing about the idea of God, without ruling him out completely.
He relates an anecdote, concerning a meeting with Pope John Paul II.

The Catholic Church had made a bad mistake with Galileo when it tried to lay down
the law on a question of science, declaring that the sun went round the earth. Now,
centuries later, it had decided to invite a number of experts to advise it on cosmology.
At the end of the conference the participants were granted an audience with the Pope.

He told us it was all right to study the evolution of the universe after the big bang, but we should not inquire into the big bang itself because that was the moment of Creation and therefore the work of God. I was glad then that he did not know the subject of the talk I had just given at the conference—the possibility that space-time was finite but had no boundary, which means that it had no beginning, no moment of creation. I had no desire to share the fate of Galileo, with whom I feel a strong sense of identity, partly because of the coincidence of having been born exactly 300 years after his death [15]

Even in this supposedly easy-to-read book of Hawking's, his ideas are difficult to follow. Like Einstein before him, his theories are famous for not being understood. His name will be very familiar to science teachers, however, and, for that matter, to their pupils. Clearly, where his views encroach on the subject of spirituality, they are going to be of interest to science teachers and will, no doubt, influence them. Unfortunately, despite his enormous reputation, his religious comments are prone to some very old chestnuts, including this comment:

Why does the universe go to all the bother of existing? Is the unified theory so compelling that it brings about its own existence? Or does it need a creator, and if so, does he have any other effect on the universe? And who created him? [16]

The last sentence of the quote seems to this author to be particularly unworthy of a deep thinker. Sarfati has shown that such a comment demonstrates a lack of logical thinking. 'The question "Who created God?" is illogical, just like "To whom is the bachelor married?"' [17] 'Who created God?' is a question which ignores the logic of definition. Sarfati continues:

The universe requires a cause because it had a *beginning*. … God, unlike the universe, had *no beginning*, so doesn't need a cause. In addition, Einstein's general relativity, which has much experimental support, shows that time is linked to matter and space. So *time itself* would have begun along with matter and space. Since God, by definition, is the creator of the whole universe, he is the creator of time. Therefore He is not limited by the time dimension He created, so has *no beginning* in time—God is 'the high and lofty One that inhabiteth eternity' (Is. 57:15). Therefore He doesn't have a cause. [18]

Chapter 6

Having committed the secular heresy of suggesting that Stephen Hawking may have committed a logical fallacy, it is worth pointing out the error of the earlier quote that I used, in which he suggests that Galileo's problems were because of the opposition of the church to true science. Although the church did oppose Galileo, this was because of their error in accepting Aristotelian views on geocentrism, rather than what the Bible actually says. Grigg illustrates this error aptly.

Many Church leaders allowed themselves to be persuaded by the Aristotelians at the universities that the geocentric (earth-centred) system was taught in Scripture and that Galileo was contradicting the Bible. They therefore bitterly opposed Galileo to the extent of forcing him on pain of death to repudiate his findings.

This was because:

1. The Church leaders had accepted as dogma the belief system of the pagan (i.e. non-Christian) philosophers, Aristotle and Ptolemy, which had become the worldview of the then scientific establishment. The result was that Church leaders were using the knowledge of the day to interpret Scripture, instead of using the Bible to evaluate the knowledge of the day.

2. They clung to the 'majority opinion' about the universe and rejected the 'minority view' of Copernicus and Galileo, even after Galileo had presented indisputable evidence based on repeatable scientific observations that the majority was wrong.

They picked out a few verses from the Bible which they thought said that the sun moved around the earth, but they failed to realize that Bible texts must be understood in terms of what the author intended to convey. Thus, when Moses wrote of the 'risen' sun and sun 'set', his purpose was not to formulate an astronomical dictum. Rather he, by God's spirit, was using the language of appearance so that his readers would easily understand what time of day he was talking about. And it is perfectly valid in physics to describe *motion relative to the most convenient reference frame*, which in this case is the earth.

3. This plain meaning (the time of day) is perfectly satisfied by the language of

appearance and does not demand the secondary deduction that it is the sun itself which moves.[19]

It cannot be over-emphasised that the argument in Galileo's day was not one of science versus the Bible, but of science versus Greek pagan philosophy.

d 'Physicists love to expound on the "scientific method" as they look down from their press-confirmed vantage point of kings of science ... Which is easier to believe in, probability or God? ... The ultimate fraud is the scientific atheist who believes in probability.' (B.Kosko)[20]

The quote from Kosko seems to put, succinctly, the supposed dichotomy between science and spirituality into context, and is therefore at the heart of the present investigation. Hoary old chestnuts were mentioned above Another example concerns the nature of probability in the universe. It is argued that every change of state or energy involves a probability function. It can indeed be shown that many physical phenomena can be observed to follow a probability function. For example, if one die is rolled, it cannot be determined if it will fall on a six. If six thousand dice are rolled, however, it is very likely that about one thousand will land on a six. The dice that have landed on a six could be removed and the remaining dice counted and shaken again. Once again, sixes are removed, and the remainder counted and shaken. A graph of dice remaining plotted against number of shakes

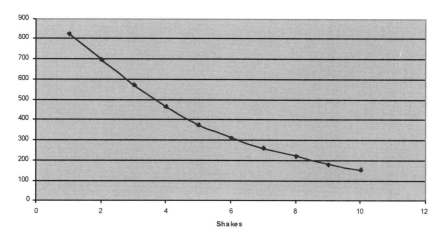

gives a regular, mathematical shape—an exponential decay, but only if the number of dice is large. Such a graph is shown below.

Radioactive decay, as an example, also follows an exponential decay curve. It can therefore be assumed that the decay of an atom of a radioactive isotope also follows a probability function. One atom is unpredictable. It might decay or it might not. However, millions of atoms (and just 12g of carbon contains $6 \cdot 023 \times 10^{23}$ atoms) will behave in a completely predictable fashion. Each individual event in the evolution of the universe is assumed to have involved a number of possibilities, one of which happened, because it was chosen randomly. The order in the universe, it could be said, is simply a macro effect, rather like the predictability of shaking a large number of dice.

The 'old chestnut' comment, then, concerns the creation of the universe. It has been said that the chances of the big bang resulting in all the universe's atoms getting together in the way that they have, producing life here on earth, is rather less probable than the chances of an explosion in a print works resulting in the creation of a dictionary. The logical fallacy involved in the probability model illustrated above is that the assumption of random, probability-driven events has to be assumed. It is therefore a presupposition. The presupposition that everything was created by God is therefore an equally logical presupposition—indeed, this author would submit that it is a superior presupposition, allowing rational explanation of far more of the scientific facts.

In analysing the various responses to Question 6, it would be convenient to divide the answers of respondents according to how they answered Question 1. The first three considered are three of the positive respondents to this question. Arthur disagrees with Dawkins. Echoing Schaeffer's comments, Arthur says that there is 'much evidence for simplicity, design, unity in physics'. He agrees with Schaeffer, adding that it is possible for ordered events to 'lead to chaotic events e.g. atom bomb exploding' but not vice versa. He does not agree with Kosko, interestingly, even though Kosko's comments seem to be in opposition to Dawkins. He says, 'Believing in probability does not preclude belief in God. When you toss a coin, its "fate" depends upon the same physical laws, which govern all events. The fact that the outcome is uncertain is because of the difficulty that *man* has in weighing up all of the factors involved. God has no such problems '

The lot is cast into the lap, But its every decision is from the LORD (Proverbs 16:33).

Brenda also disagrees with Dawkins and agrees with Schaeffer. Of Dawkins's comment, Brenda says 'This is purely a non-spiritual, pro-scientific criticism of life itself.' She also disagrees with Hawking, but qualifies this by saying, 'Curiously, this gives the promise of a creator, but only when the time was right.' The issue of order is raised again in Brenda's response to Kosko, quoting the comment often attributed to Einstein: 'God doesn't play dice.'

Deborah's comments display a similar pattern. Deborah disagrees with Dawkins. 'Humans have free will and consciousness. We can ignore our DNA.' Her last comment would be worth exploring further—the issue of whether DNA can really be over-ridden by free will, but the fact that Deborah believes it is of interest. She adds, in agreement to Schaeffer's comment, 'There does seem to be order, especially in human minds.' Deborah is also critical of Hawking's comment. 'It seems a rather confused argument. It depends on what you mean by God's creative act.'

The comments of those who answered negatively to question 1 are now considered. Colin, Eric and Fiona, as examples of these respondents, all agree with Dawkins. Colin qualifies agreement by saying, 'There must be moral guidance in every lesson where appropriate.' He also agrees with Schaeffer, saying, 'all societies have a degree of order.' The reason for this apparent contradiction is made clear by Colin's agreement with Hawking: 'I am agnostic and I believe there is sufficient doubt linked to [Hawking's] statement.'

Eric agrees with Dawkins, saying, 'I think we try to create good and destroy evil but we define what they are.' Eric disagrees with Schaeffer. 'There are so many examples of chaos.' This comment is seemingly contradicted by Eric's agreement with Hawking, saying that 'there must have been a "manufacture process" to make the earth. It is not clear how such a "manufacture process" could have developed, alongside a belief in chaos. However, his avowed atheism is qualified by a positive response to

Kosko: 'There is so much which cannot be explained by scientific method.'

Fiona agrees with Dawkins, but makes no response to Schaeffer. In response to Hawking, Fiona says, 'Speculation about what happened before the "known" history of the universe seems pointless.'

Teachers who responded to the questionnaire have produced thoughtful contributions. Many science teachers do have a religious faith and allow this to influence the way they teach. The key question seems to be question 5, where those respondents who do not think that their values should influence their teaching of a topic, nevertheless admit that it probably happens. The expected response to question 6 was 'disagree, agree, disagree, agree' for those with religious belief and 'agree, disagree, agree, disagree' for those without. The fact that the answers were more complex than this suggests that there is a considerable amount of influence of spiritual ideas, though some teachers would not use the word spiritual to identify it.

Notes

1 **C.S. Lewis,** *Miracles* (London: Collins, 1947).

2 **F.A. Schaeffer,** *Escape from Reason* (London: Inter-Varsity Press, 1968).

3 Since the completion of this analysis, I have received some comments by email, in response to some of these questions being posted on my web site. It has not been possible to determine which country these comments have come from, so they are not included in the present survey. However, it is interesting to note that most of the comments have come from atheists or agnostics, who, nevertheless, believe that there should be a spiritual dimension to science teaching. This is all the more surprising, since the author's web site is advertised only through the Christian media or other Christian web sites.

4 The government department responsible for education has changed its name many times during my teaching career. When I began teaching, it was the Department of Education and Science (DES), then becoming the Department for Education (DfE), the Department for Education and Employment (DfEE) and now the Department for Education and Skills (DfES). Prior to devolution in 1999, education issues in Wales were determined by the DfE, but administered by the Welsh Office (WO). After devolution, education policy for Wales was separated from that of England and operated by the Welsh Assembly Government Ministry for Education and Lifelong Learning.

5 It should go without saying that all teachers' names in this study are pseudonyms, chosen in alphabetical order. The only information about the teacher concerned that the names actually convey is the teacher's gender.

6 **M. Roques,** *Curriculum Unmasked, Towards a Christian Understanding of Education* (Eastbourne: Monarch, 1989), p. 210.

7 Ibid. p. 210.

8 **R. Dawkins,** *River out of Eden* (London: Phoenix, 1995), p. 133.

9 **F. Schaeffer,** *Genesis in Space and Time* (London: Hodder and Stoughton, 1973), p. 58.

10 Ibid. p. 58.

11 Ibid. p. 59.

12 **F. Schaeffer,** *Escape from Reason* (London: Inter-Varsity Press, 1968), p. 87.

13 Quoted on an online site of Richard Dawkins's quotes:
http://en.thinkexist.com/quotes/richard_dawkin.

14 **S.W. Hawking,** *A Brief History of Time* (London: Transworld, 1988), p.9.

15 Ibid. p. 174.

16 Ibid.

17 **J. Sarfati,** *If God created the universe, then who created God?*, TJ **12**(1):20–22 April 1998.

18 Ibid.

19 **R. Grigg,** *The Galileo 'Twist'*, Creation **19**(4):30–32, September 1997.

20 **Bart Kosko,** *Fuzzy Thinking, the New Science of Fuzzy Logic* (New York: Hyperion, 1993).

Some thoughts from the research

Eureka experiences

Listening to great music is a spiritual experience for many people. The writing of this chapter, for example, was originally undertaken with J.S. Bach's magnificent St Matthew Passion in the background. It is generally accepted, even by those of his fans who are atheists, that for Bach's music to be fully appreciated, one must be aware of the faith that influenced it. The late Douglas Adams said that 'the fact that I think Bach was mistaken [with regards to religion] doesn't alter the fact that I think the B minor Mass is one of the great pinnacles of human achievement. It still absolutely moves me to tears to hear it. I find the whole business of religion profoundly interesting. But it does mystify me that otherwise intelligent people take it seriously.'[1] However, what mystified Adams was seen by others as essential to the understanding of the music. Another commentator said:

Some people ... fail to understand [Bach's] music because they have conditioned their ears to the musical slang of other types which make no attempt to bespeak the native beauty of the Gospel as did the music of Bach. The problem is not merely a cultural or a musical problem; it is likewise, and just as forcefully, a spiritual problem.[2]

The problem, to which the above commentator refers, is probably in some way analogous to the present study. It is the contention of this study that science and spirituality are inseparable, and that, therefore, science education must address at least some of the issues of spirituality which pertain to science.

To continue the above analogy which has linked music to spirituality, a little further, it has been noted by some that a link has been forged between music and an understanding of the origins of the universe. Leaver says in his book, *Music as Preaching,* that:

Imaginative authors, when dealing with the 'theological' question of cosmic origins, have to resort to music to explain the significance of what was involved.[3]

One such imaginative author, J.R.R. Tolkein, in his masterful account of the creation of Middle Earth, allowed his imagination to state:

There was Eru, the One ... and he made first the Ainur, the Holy Ones ... And he spoke to them, propounding to them themes of music; and they sang before him, and he was glad.[4]

The use of music as an analogy to creation seems to emphasise the religious or spiritual nature of considering the universe. As God says to Job:

Where were you when I laid the foundations of the earth? Tell Me, if you have understanding. Who determined its measurements? Surely you know Or who stretched the line upon it? To what were its foundations fastened? Or who laid its cornerstone, When the morning stars sang together, And all the sons of God shouted for joy. (Job 38:4–7)

The song of the morning stars accompanies the creation, according to the book of Job. The writer of the book of Job is considering matters, which might today be considered in the scientific realm. However, he is addressing the experience as spiritual, and accompanying it with song.

Thompson, a physicist who has written on the ways in which our understanding of the material world is influenced by spirituality, in a brief description, which beautifully describes what many feel, compares music to quantum physics.

The song is like a particle of feeling, unique in the trajectory of its rise and fall as it inscribes in time the story of the emotional forces by which it is buffeted and impelled ... The dance is like a wave-motion, a communication of energy between individuals, filling space with a field of force.[5]

This sense of spiritual experience, akin to listening to great music, has a practical outworking. In the classroom, a pupil's feelings of pleasure or boredom are linked to the potential for progress in the subject. The good teacher will attempt to engage the pupil's enthusiasm. In science teaching, this is frequently achieved by creating a sense of wonder, for example, in the microscopic world of atoms or the macroscopic world of stars and galaxies. Is it for this reason that pupils are taken on trips to planetaria, to see the universe unfolding over their heads, learning facts, which could have been gleaned from the physics text book? It is presumably hoped that the environment into which the pupils are being taken will *inspire* them as well as *teach* them. Implicit in the promotion of such experience is the spiritual notion of one's place in the universe—an awareness which gives in turn a sense of proportion or a sense of wonder.

For an example of this process, we may turn to the pupil who was struggling with the idea of ionic bonding. Why did magnesium chloride have the formula $MgCl_2$? Why was it two chloride ions to one magnesium ion? Gradually, she began to understand the principle of full outer orbitals: that Mg needed to lose two electrons, but Cl only wanted one. She then understood that there would have to be a second Cl atom to take the extra electron. This is a lesson that the author has taught many times, but on this occasion the pupil's face was aglow with a sense of real discovery. 'It all makes sense' she exclaimed, when clearly ten minutes earlier it had made no sense at all. We might ask if it is fair to suggest that such a *eureka* moment is a religious experience. Certainly it has similarities. The subject matter was not that important; what was important was the realisation that these science lessons could actually make sense. This was something that apparently changed that young lady's outlook on life. Here again we return to the concept of spirituality as 'the recognition of what is going on', referred to in our third chapter.

Poole suggests some typical statements which illustrate common misconceptions about science, e.g. the assumptions that science:

… is based on fixed laws which govern how the natural world must behave and, in view of this, miracles are impossible.

... deals with facts, with realities such as atoms, whereas religion is about father-figures and old-men-in-the-sky.[6]

Since these views are widespread, they must have come from somewhere. And since both views are simply wrong, should they not be challenged in the classroom by the science teacher?

A less controversial example of wrong assumptions might further illustrate the point being made. Suppose there are two spoons stuck into a serving of ice cream in a dish. One spoon is aluminium, the other is plastic. Pupils are then asked, 'Which spoon is the colder?' Invariably, pupils answer that the aluminium spoon is the colder. 'Metals are colder than plastic,' one of the author's pupils boldly asserted. So the teacher fetches thermometers, which are strapped to the spoons. Minutes later, it is discovered that both spoons are the same temperature. Even faced with this incontrovertible evidence, it is still difficult for some of the pupils to accept that their presuppositional bias is wrong. Of course, the aluminium spoon merely *feels* colder, because it is a better conductor of heat than plastic. There is a difference in temperature between the experimenter's fingers (approx. 37 degrees Celcius) and the ice cream (approx. 0 degrees), so that a flow of heat is caused through *both* spoons. Heat travels faster through conductors than insulators, so the fingers feel a quicker heat loss when touching the aluminium spoon than when touching the plastic spoon. It is this faster movement of heat out of the experimenter's fingers which causes the aluminium spoon to *feel* colder than the plastic spoon.

If clearly factual situations like this can cause problems, how much more the problems that arise in what some people would term as grey areas. For example, suppose the second of Poole's comments, quoted above, is deconstructed. 'Science deals with facts.' That statement is itself fraught with difficulties. Was Newtonian physics a 'fact' before Einstein suggested something better? 'Realities such as atoms'—this author has often teased pupils by asking them if they have ever seen an atom. Of course, we can observe the effects produced by atoms, and books can publish images of atoms produced by, for example, electron microscopes, but has any average school pupil actually seen an atom? The pupils are expected to take the teacher's word for it that atoms actually exist. The fact that most pupils will believe the teacher has vast implications for more controversial areas of the curriculum—such as, has any pupil seen one kind of animal evolve into a completely different kind of animal, by the spontaneous generation of new genetic information?

Poole claims that teaching atomic theory as fact is 'ontological reductionism'.

Ontological reductionism ... claims that the atom-and-molecule story is the only valid description—or, at any rate, the best description—of any phenomenon under question.7

This attitude is implicit in some of the comments in chapter 6, such as the comments of the respondent Fiona in response to the quotation from Hawking, i.e. 'Speculation about what happened before the "known" history of the universe seems pointless.' Poole continues:

There is a half-truth in this idea of a 'best' description, but it must be made clear 'best for what?'8

On the limitations of science, he says:

Pupils need to realise that the methods and test procedures of science systematically miss out matters like beauty, goodness and God. The limitations of science are methodological, not territorial. This means that, whereas all physical phenomena can *in principle* be examined scientifically, the range of questions which can be answered is limited by the kinds of questions asked within science. These include 'How?' and 'When?' questions about the natural world, but do not embrace questions about plan or purpose. An understanding of the limitations of science as a mode of inquiry should form an intrinsic part of a science education programme.9

Followed to its natural conclusion, Poole seems to imply that science is the domain of the question 'How?' while religion is the domain of the question 'Why?' This is a common misconception. Although science is notoriously bad at addressing the question 'Why?' it must be noted that the early chapters of Genesis do not address the question 'Why?' either. Genesis 1 never states *why* God made the world, only indicating *how* it was made. The 'Why' question is addressed elsewhere in the Bible—for example, see Psalm 97:6: 'The heavens declare His righteousness, And all the peoples see His glory.' Genesis 1, however, reads like a statement of scientific fact— and that, of course, is how this author accepts it.

It is worth noting that Poole's comments were written in 1986 in response to a consultative document, published by the Secondary Science Curriculum Review, entitled *Science Education 11–16*. This document was the precursor to the '*Science in the National Curriculum*' documents. This book originated as a dissertation, being written some twelve years later, and yet the last sentence of Poole's comments quoted above has still not come to fruition in a major way. Many schemes of work still pay no more than lip service to the National Curriculum comments on Scientific Enquiry.

These studies have shown that there is a need for the link between spirituality and science to be acknowledged and acted upon. It has been shown that the link exists, but is not largely understood by classroom science teachers. It is suggested, therefore, that five propositions could be addressed, which might improve the situation somewhat, in order that this issue is recognised much more widely as having a significant import for all science teaching. They are, in a sense, the crystallisation of the research in this work. More drastic surgery, however, is suggested in the next chapter.

Five propositions

1. SHORT COMMENTARIES ON *SCIENTIFIC ENQUIRY* ISSUES, ON THE SECTION 'IDEAS AND EVIDENCE IN SCIENCE'

It has been observed that one of the problems with understanding how to tackle this subject is the lack of clear guidance as to what the writers of the National curriculum, or the Department for Education and Skills, mean by what they have published. Humpty Dumpty told Alice that words meant whatever he wanted them to mean, but it is clear that science teachers need more guidance than that. The issue at stake is whether the DfES take the view that the preamble to the Programme of Study is simply a collection of worthy words or whether they form the basis of a policy statement on which they expect educationalists to act. If, as it is to be hoped, it is the latter, then some expansion of thought on the matter would be of immeasurable help to the classroom teacher.

The National Curriculum clearly stated that 'Pupils should be taught … ways in which scientific work may be affected by the contexts in which it takes place [for example, social, historical, moral and spiritual], and how these contexts may affect whether or not ideas are accepted.'[10] As previously observed, the material in the square brackets is optional and exemplary. Nevertheless, when I was a teacher I was told by a school inspector that such bracketed material is still fair game for any questions that the pupils may be asked on that section. It follows that it is acceptable for pupils to be examined on ways in which scientific work may be affected by spiritual contexts.

2. POLICIES ON *IDEAS AND EVIDENCE IN SCIENCE* NEED TO BE INCLUDED IN SCIENCE DEPARTMENTS' HANDBOOKS

The importance of issues to a science department can often be gauged by its prominence in the department's handbook. Policies on access to the curriculum, equal opportunities, health and safety, language, the Curriculum Cymreig and information technology can usually be found in such documents (at least the abbreviation Curr. Cym. is often to be seen in department handbooks in Wales). It is against this background that it is suggested that if *ideas and evidence in science* is considered valuable by the DfES, then policies for its implementation need to be included in the Departmental Handbook and should be looked for by school inspectors.

3. MATERIAL ADDRESSING SCIENCE IN A SPIRITUAL CONTEXT NEEDS TO BE INCLUDED IN SCHEMES OF WORK

At a management seminar in 1997, arranged for new and prospective heads of science, I was was advised on the creation of schemes of work. One model included a column headed *Opportunities*. This column was used to point out to the teacher which activities lent themselves to cross-curricular themes; for example, opportunities to use ICT, opportunities to mention something pertaining to Wales (to fulfil the demands of the Curriculum Cymreig), etc. Such a column could also contain instances of when a topic lends itself to the teaching of spiritual science. Such a column can ensure that individual teachers address such issues.

4. SCIENCE TEACHERS NEED TO ADOPT A QUESTIONING STYLE IN LESSONS WHICH ALLOWS AND ENCOURAGES PUPILS TO THINK BEYOND THE 'SCIENCE AS FACT' PHILOSOPHIES

For teachers who are unduly worried about influencing pupils towards a particular philosophy against their will, it needs to be pointed out that most schools have a *hidden curriculum*. Certain values are expected to be taught by example in the classroom. These include values such as respect for teachers, for each other and for property, values of industry and endeavour, and values of punctuality and reliability. Science teachers would also be teaching values of experimentation and the means of carrying out investigations. It is not far beyond this to encourage teachers to encourage pupils to think beyond the so-called factual boundaries of science. That there is a creative value in the questioning attitude is a presumption of scientific advance and it is certainly not incompatible with the questioning attitude required for successful investigative techniques.

Although the idea that pupils should ask questions is fundamental to science teaching, it would appear to break down when the topic turns to *origins* science. Frequently, pupils are not encouraged to question aspects of evolutionary theory, or the Big Bang, and are taught it as if it is fact. It is always better, in my opinion, to train pupils to question any scientific 'fact'.

5. CONSIDERATION OF THESE ISSUES MUST FIND A PLACE IN TEACHER TRAINING PROGRAMMES

The next generation of science teachers ought to 'stand on the shoulders' of the present ones. If teachers are going to be able to lead pupils along this road of self-discovery, beyond the factual boundaries, then the seeds of the ideas must be sown in the schools of education. Studies made in teacher training colleges of National Curriculum Science must not omit the area of *ideas and evidence in science*. It would be inconceivable for science student teachers to be untrained as far as *health and safety* is concerned. *Ideas and evidence in science*, including all that has been said herein about science, in its spiritual context, has been given equal prominence in National Curriculum Science. These issues, therefore, must be addressed by the next generation of teachers.

It is suggested that these five propositions would at least begin to address the communication of these ideas to the pupils; ideas that embrace the reality that science is not everything, nor is there necessarily an as yet undiscovered scientific explanation for everything. Some things are beyond science. Some science is beyond what is currently known as science. Many 'real' scientists understand this. School pupils are being trained to be 'real' scientists. They need to be made aware that the scientific world is bigger than they may have imagined.

Notes

1   **D. Adams,** *The Salmon of Doubt* (New York: Harmony Books, 2002), p. xxvii.

2   **W.E. Buszin,** 'Lutheran Theology as Reflected in the Life and Works of J.S. Bach' in *Concordia Theological Monthly*, Vol. 21, pp. 896–923.

3   **R.A. Leaver,** *Music as Preaching* (Latimer House, 1982), p. 4.

4   **J.R.R. Tolkein,** *The Silmarillion* (George Allen & Unwin, 1977), p. 15.

5   **R. Thompson,** *The Spirituality of Matter* (London: SPCK, 1990), p.168.

6   **M.W. Poole,** 'Science education and the interplay between science and religion' in *School Science Review*, 1985, 239, **67**, 252–261 (London: Association for Science Education).

7   Ibid. p. 255.

8   Ibid. p. 255.

9   Ibid. p. 256.

10 *Science: The National Curriculum for England* (1999) p. 46.

Truth and lies in education

Much of this work has been fairly circumspect, in reference to the sort of science that is currently taught in state schools. However, this chapter will explore some more serious issues, and some more controversial issues. The chapter title contains the word 'lies'. What should one call it if pupils are taught something which is factually incorrect? Whose fault is it if the pupil picks up factually incorrect information? Is the information factually incorrect because of deliberate policy or by accident?

There could be any number of answers to these questions. It is to be hoped that all teachers will want their pupils to be taught what is factually correct. If there are controversial areas, it is to be hoped that teachers will want their pupils to be appraised of all sides of the argument.

If factually incorrect information is presented to the children, it could be for a number of reasons. It could be because the teacher has made a genuine mistake. It could be because science knowledge has moved on, and the teacher was not aware of new knowledge. It could be because information in a text book is incorrect. It could be because the instructions in a syllabus are incorrect. This chapter includes examples of all of these.

If there is factually incorrect science being taught to pupils, should we start to discuss the issue of blame? For example, if the teacher is not aware that science has moved on since their lessons were planned, whose fault is that? Is it the fault of the Local Education Authority, or the school's senior management team, or board of governors—should it be their responsibility to account for their staff's knowledge? Is it the fault of the teacher? Should it be mandatory for teachers to keep themselves up to date with the latest scientific research? How should they go about doing this? Who is going to assess that they have achieved in this area?

Examination of error

It will not be possible to examine every instance of error being taught in science classrooms today. We will therefore restrict ourselves to a number of case studies. In the selection of these case studies we need to be fair.

- I will not be picking on individual teachers. Science teachers are hardworking individuals who need support. It is not possible for such a teacher to be up to date with all the latest aspects of scientific research, especially if they are teaching outside their normal area of expertise—a common problem among UK science teachers. We will therefore restrict ourselves to published materials such as text books and syllabuses.
- Some supposed errors may be controversial. As a creationist, I believe evolutionary theory as a whole to be unscientific. However, it makes more sense to restrict my case studies to concepts or 'facts' which have been accepted as erroneous by evolutionists themselves
- Some errors may be honest mistakes. We will therefore restrict ourselves to cases where the published work appears many years after the concept or 'fact' concerned had been shown to be in error. Published works appearing five years or so after such a discovery should have been updated, including those works which are revisions of earlier works. While individual school science teachers may have difficulty in being up-to date within five years, this should pose no problem to the authors and publishers of text books and examination curricula, who have a responsibility to check the accuracy of their works.

Readers of this book will be interested to know where these errors are being taught. If it is true that not all science teachers can keep up to date with the latest scientific research, then how much less likely is it that ordinary parents know what errors their children are being taught? It may be an eye-opener to many parents to see which popular 'icons' of scientific theories are, in fact, known to be incorrect.

Peppered moths

Peppered moths are usually taught as an example of natural selection. Sometimes this is expanded to identify the moths as an example of evolution in practice. The BBC takes the latter view, using peppered moths on their 'GCSE Bitesize' website.[1] This website provides revision assistance for children sitting General Certificate of Secondary Education exams.

The alleged support for natural selection given by peppered moths is aptly described in one current GCSE biology text book.

The common form is speckled but there is also a variety which is black. The black variety was rare in 1850, but by 1895 in the Manchester area its numbers had risen to 98 per cent of the population of peppered moths. Observation showed that the light variety was concealed better than the dark variety when they rested on tree-trunks covered with lichens. In the Manchester area, pollution had caused the death of the lichens and the darkening of the tree-trunks with soot. In this industrial area the dark variety was the better camouflaged (hidden) of the two and was not picked off so often by birds.[2]

It should be noticed that Mackean describes this as an example of natural selection, whereas the BBC claims it is an example of evolution. Mackean is correct—if these experiments were genuine, they would imply a reduction in genetic information, not an increase. Evolution requires an increase in genetic information.

Using the language of evolution, a recent A-Level biology text book says:

Clearly the darker moth has a selective advantage over the light moth in industrial areas, whereas in non-polluted areas this advantage is with the light moth.[3]

The same A-Level book includes a map of the UK showing the distribution of peppered moths of light and dark varieties. This map is reproduced here.

In his textbook, Williams does not comment on the observation that there is a high concentration of dark-variety moths in rural East Anglia— a result which flies in the face of the usual interpretation of the observed data. Conversely, dark moths are rare in South Wales, even though this was an area of high pollution when the experiments were carried out.

The alleged principles shown by peppered moths are considered educationally very important. They are included as examples in many GCSE science and biology syllabuses. One current GCSE biology syllabus states: 'Candidates should be able to … describe how the process of natural selection may result in … changes within a species, *as illustrated by the peppered moth*.'[4] (emphasis mine)

Evolution

Most biologists believe that natural selection, among other processes, contributes to the evolution of new species and that the great variety of living organisms on the Earth is the product of millions of years of evolution, involving natural selection (p. 205).

The peppered moth

A possible example of natural selection is provided by a species of moth called the peppered moth. The common form is speckled but there is also a variety

This condition has already been mentioned on p. 19_. A person with sickle-cell disease has inherited bo__ recessive alleles (Hb^5Hb^5) for defective haemoglob__ The distortion and destruction of the red cells wh__ occurs in low oxygen concentrations leads to bouts __ severe anaemia (Figure 23.8). In many African cou__ tries, sufferers have a reduced chance of reaching rep__ ductive age and having a family. There is thu__ selection pressure which tends to remove the homo__ gous recessives from the population. In such a case, __ might expect the harmful Hb^5 allele to be selected __ of the population altogether. However, the hete__

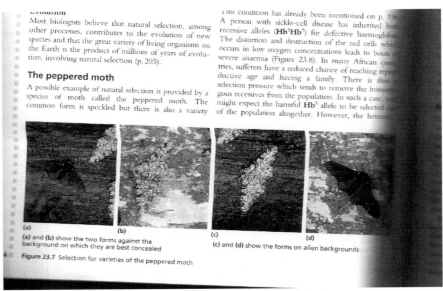

(a) and (b) show the two forms against the background on which they are best concealed

(c) and (d) show the forms on alien backgrounds

Figure 23.7 Selection for varieties of the peppered moth

Peppered moths photographs in Mackean's GCSE Biology

The observations about peppered moths were carried out initially in the 1950s by Bernard Kettlewell. Unfortunately, his observations should carry a 'health-warning' Peppered moths do not, as a rule, rest on the trunks of trees, so the main premise is flawed. It turns out that the famous photographs, used in so many text books, are fraudulent. Some photos are taken using dead moths glued or pinned to the trunks. Others use live specimens which are placed by hand on the trunks. In daylight the moths are drowsy and tend to stay where they are put. The moths actually tend to rest hidden under the leaf canopy, rather than in the open on the trunk.

Criticisms of Kettlewell's experiments first emerged in the 1980s— twenty years ago. In 1998, Professor Jerry Coyne of the University of Chicago said that finding out the moth story was wrong was like when he found out at age six that it was actually his father who was bringing the Christmas presents.[5] Coyne has not been pleased that his remarks have been quoted by creationists, such as this author, but the genie is out. Other

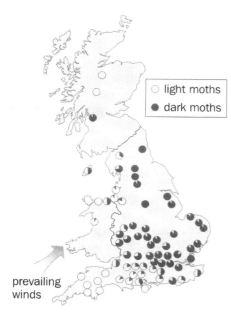

light moths
dark moths

prevailing
winds

*The proportions of light and dark moths
found in Britain today*

Moth Distribution from Williams

biologists have admitted to gluing specimens to trees to take some of the iconic textbook photos.

Kettlewell said that if Darwin had seen his experiments 'he would have witnessed the consummation and confirmation of his life's work'.[6] What we now find is that science textbooks and syllabuses in the UK (and, judging from my correspondence, America too) are basing their evidence for evolution on something that has been known to be a fraud for twenty years. What word can we use to describe the situation, if our children are knowingly being taught something which is not true? It is a source of considerable amazement to this author that Michael Majarus, who lectures on evolution at the University of Cambridge, can ask himself, in view of all the errors, whether the peppered moth story should still be taught in schools, and answers himself: 'The answer is an unequivocal "yes". The basic story is easy to understand.'[7]

To such people, the fact that the example is 'easy to understand' is more important than whether it is actually true.

The use of fossils

The Science National Curriculum in England states:

Pupils should be taught that the fossil record is evidence for evolution. (Sc2.4i)[8]

A very similar statement appears in the National Curriculum in Wales (Sc2.4.9).[9]

These statements are interpreted in the OCR biology GCSE thus.

Candidates should be able to explain briefly how organisms may have become fossilised and recognize that fossils provide evidence for evolution.[10]

The use of the fossil record is controversial. Many creationists would point out that the fossil record actually shows stasis[11] and extinction, not evolution. Indeed, each fossil is a static snapshot in time rather than a record of change.

This section of one chapter of this book cannot be expected to be a comprehensive analysis of fossils and fossilization. Others have provided much more detailed information.[12] What our present study will confine itself to is the analysis of clearly factually incorrect statements. The statement that 'the fossil record is evidence for evolution' is factually incorrect. Indeed, the fossil record is frequently used by creationists as evidence *against* evolution.

For example, it is usually assumed that fossils take a very long time to

Fossil of a small fish being eaten by a larger fish

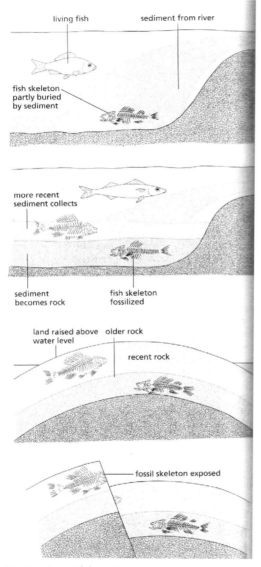

living fish

sediment from river

fish skeleton
partly buried
by sediment

more recent
sediment collects

sediment
becomes rock

fish skeleton
fossilized

land raised above
water level

older rock

recent rock

fossil skeleton exposed

Formation of fossils
according to evolution

form. However, the existence of fossil jellyfish[13] shows that at least some fossils must have happened rapidly. In fact, it is the contention of creation scientists that most fossils are produced rapidly. In the case of jellyfish, we are familiar with examples washed up on the beach. These creatures do not remain on the beach long—they quickly dry up leaving no trace in a matter of hours. Therefore, in order for fossil jellyfish to exist, the jellyfish must have been covered by sediment very quickly.

Another example of a fossil produced quickly is the fish eating a smaller fish.[14]

If the larger fish had died, it is unlikely that the smaller fish would have stayed in the bigger fish's mouth. The fossilization must have occurred very rapidly so that this 'snapshot' of marine life could happen.

There is a classic textbook illustration of how marine fossils occurred. In the illustration shown to the left, taken from Mackean's GCSE biology textbook mentioned

Observed death and decay of fish

Fossil fish are the result of rapid burial

earlier, we see two fish in the first frame. One of these has died and sunk to the bottom of the river. Over a period of time, river sediment gradually covers the fossil. This is then uplifted by slow earth movements, and then exposed by faulting.

Any fisherman knows that this is not what happens to fish when they die. The following amusing illustration gives a better understanding of what happens to dead fish. They do not sink—they float.

It is much more likely that a fish fossil is produced by sudden covering by sediment.

Such a scenario is consistent with the creationist view that most fossils were formed in the Flood. However, school textbooks continue to teach children a method of fossilisation which is demonstrably erroneous.

Notes

1 Examples of Evolution 1,
   http://www.bbc.co.uk/schools/gcsebitesize/biology/variationandinheritance/3evolutionrev5.shtml.

Chapter 8

2 **D.G. Mackean,** GCSE Biology (third edition, 2002) (London: John Murray (Publishers) Ltd, p. 204.

3 **G. Williams** (2000), *Advanced Biology for You* (Cheltenham: Nelson Thornes), p. 377.

4 OCR GCSE in Biology, 2000, p. 38.

5 **J.A. Coyne,** *Nature* **396**(6706):35–36.

6 **H. Kettlewell** (1959), 'Darwin's missing evidence' in *Evolution and the fossil record, readings from Scientific American* (San Francisco: W.H. Freeman and Co., 1978), p. 23.

7 **M.E.N. Majerus,** 'The Peppered Moth: a problem not to be sneezed at', *Biologist* **53**(1), pp. 13–16, Feb 2006.

8 *Science: The National Curriculum for England* (QCA, 1999), p. 50.

9 *Science in the National Curriculum in Wales* (English Language Version), (ACCAC, 2000), p. 49.

10 OCR GCSE in Biology, 2000, p. 38.

11 In biological terms, *stasis* implies that no change over time is seen.

12 See, for example, **C. Wieland,** *Stones and Bones* (Green Forest, AR: Master Books, 1990); **D. Gish,** *Evolution: The Fossils Still Say No* (San Diego: ICR, 1985), or, specifically on the subject of human fossils, **M. Lubenow,** *Bones of Contention* (Grand Rapids: Baker Book House, 2004).

13 D. Catchpoole, *Hundreds of Fossil Jellyfish*, *Creation* **25**(4):32–33, September 2003.

14 This fossil is on display at the Answers in Genesis **Creation Museum**, in northern Kentucky, due to open in 2007.

Scientism in the classroom

The examples in the previous chapter can be shown to be definite errors. In this chapter, I want to demonstrate how an evolutionary worldview has come to dominate the educational world. We see this in the teaching of science. Surprisingly, and alarmingly, we see this influence more and more in other curriculum areas.

Scientism is defined by Webster's dictionary as 'an exaggerated trust in the efficacy of the methods of natural science applied to all areas of investigation'. True science is no threat to those who are unafraid of the implications of Christian faith in the arena of science education. Scientism, however, masquerades as true science. It is the false idea that science is the only genuine area of knowledge. It is scientism, therefore, and not true science, which claims that all hypotheses reliant on spiritual or supernatural explanations are to be removed from science education. Such a claim is outside the proper limitations of scientific methodology.

In chapter 7 above, it was seen that genuine scientific methodology breaks down in the discussion of *origins* science. It is necessary, therefore, to define what we mean by *origins* science, and we will attempt this by defining the opposite first.

Operational science is that science which corresponds to scientific methodology. It is the sort of science carried out in laboratories or in field work. It involves the collection of data, measurements and observations. This data is reported, and is reproducible and verifiable. It is operational science that has put people on the Moon, solved the human genome sequence and created the Internet.

Origins science (sometimes referred to as *historical* science) is concerned with statements about how the world came to be. Evolutionary theory falls naturally into this category. Origins science, by definition, is not reproducible nor is it verifiable. Statements of origins science depend on the presuppositions of the scientist.

It is an obvious statement that no scientist was present at the time of the Big Bang. What is often not so obvious to people is the level of rejection of Big Bang theories, not just among creationists like me, but also by secular physicists.[1] Many of the statements, thought by the public to be factual, are the result of extrapolation by Big Bang theorists of observations made by optical instruments such as the Hubble Space Telescope. The observations are real, but the interpretation of the data relies on the presuppositions of the scientists. The danger of such interpretations being reported as fact is illustrated in Lerner's article in *New Scientist,* signed by over thirty leading physicists.

Even observations are now interpreted through this biased filter, judged right or wrong depending on whether or not they support the big bang. So discordant data on red shifts, lithium and helium abundances, and galaxy distribution, among other topics, are ignored or ridiculed. This reflects a growing dogmatic mindset that is alien to the spirit of free scientific enquiry.[2]

There should be no objection to scientists making such extrapolations, so long as their presuppositions are recognised. Different presuppositions will lead to different interpretations. Of course, not all interpretations are valid. Some presuppositions can be demonstrated to be erroneous. This is increasingly becoming the case with the Big Bang theory, for example.[3]

It is of particular concern to this study to highlight examples of where statements are addressed to children as if they were factual, when in reality they are based on presuppositions. In other words, our concern is with the confusion of operational and origins science.

The confusion of these two modes of scientific thought can be seen in the following rhetorical question by evolutionary atheist, Professor Richard Dawkins.

How do we know that the earth is four and a half billion years old and that it orbits the sun that nourishes it?[4]

The quote contains two separate statements. The second, '[the earth] orbits the sun that nourishes it', is *operational* science. It is based on reproducible, verifiable observations. The first, 'the earth is four and a half billion years old', is *origins* science. It is not reproducible, and is based only on presuppositions. The measurements used for the calculation of dates *are* reproducible—but these measurements are *interpreted* in order to arrive at the dates. Dawkins is a past master at the confusion of operational and origins science. The viewer, on hearing the above quote, might have been led to assume, incorrectly, that both parts of the sentence have equal scientific validity.

For the purposes of this study, therefore, it is not a concern to us if a textbook or syllabus claims, for example, a large age for a rock sample, and then goes on to explain, with assumptions, how the age was calculated. If textbook writers are honest about their assumptions, then this is to be welcomed. However, this is not usually the way such matters are presented. Where a statement of presupposition is presented to children as if it were a statement of fact, we have a problem to which we should object.

We need to examine this inbuilt bias in the curriculum, first in the three traditional school science areas of physics, chemistry and biology, and then in other curriculum areas. Unless otherwise stated, quotations from the National Curriculum documents for England and Wales will be from Key Stage 4 (Double Award) of the National Curriculum Programmes of Study.

Physics
Three potential areas of concern are visible in the Science National Curriculum for England document.

Pupils should be taught:
The Earth and Beyond
4.4c—how stars evolve over a long timescale
4.4d—about some ideas used to explain the origin and evolution of the universe
Radioactivity
4.6f—some uses of radioactivity, including radioactive dating of rocks[5]

(These statements are also found in the National Curriculum for Wales, items 4.4.3, 4.4.4 and 4.5.6).[6] Of these, 4.4d and 4.6f should cause no problem, if taught correctly. The statements, as written in the National Curriculum (NC), do not imply a single hypothesis. 4.4d refers to 'some ideas' in the plural. The word 'evolution', in the context of astrophysics, ought to be replaced by 'development'. Similarly, our concern with radiometric dating is with the interpretation of the results, and extrapolation into the past, not with the experimental techniques or their uses.

In the case of item 4.4c, it is not the word 'evolve' that causes concern. Astronomical evolution need not be defined in terms of increasing information, as is the case with biological evolution. However, the use of the word is likely to cause confusion, and is probably included to imply an acceptance of Big Bang cosmology. A qualification is surely needed, however, for the phrase 'a long timescale'. The use of that phrase is problematic. We can guess at the presupposition of the NC writers. It is unlikely that they considered 6,000 years to be their long timescale. Even with this item, however, it would be possible to teach in a plural manner, as some of the current creationist models allow for the appearance of millions of years of stellar development, while the normal six days of creation took place on earth. Nevertheless, the item would be better worded as 'how stars are thought by some to have changed over a long timescale'.

In the interpretation of any NC items, it ought to be axiomatic that writers of syllabuses consider Sc1.1b, 'how scientific controversies can arise from different ways of interpreting empirical evidence'. (Item Sc1.1.4 in Wales.) In practice, however, this item is usually only referenced with respect to known contemporary controversies, such as the siting of wind farms, or a discussion of global warming. Rarely is Sc1.1b invoked in the context of genuine scientific disagreement.

Two typical GCSE syllabuses have been examined, to check their application of these items. For English schools, the Oxford, Cambridge and RSA (OCR) Double Award Linear Science has been used, while for Wales, the equivalent Welsh Joint Education Committee (WJEC) document was used. In both cases, the statements referring to radiometric dating are non-problematic. For example, the OCR syllabus simply states, on page 66, that 'candidates should be able to ... explain how measurements of the amounts of radioactive elements and their decay products in rocks can be used to calculate the age of a rock'. Another statement, referring to Sc4.6f, is that 'candidates should be able to ... apply an understanding of half-life to explain why different sources are suited to particular purposes'. The WJEC syllabus states that 'candidates should … understand how radioactivity can be used to find the age of rocks'. Neither syllabus presents the slightest doubt.

It is right for students to be taught an appreciation of how the radiometric calculations are undertaken. However, an application of Sc1.1b ought to lead teachers to encourage students to recognise and challenge the presuppositions used in the calculations. Such criticism rarely occurs, and is not encouraged by the text books. Johnson's popular GCSE Physics text book[7] does not mention that assumptions are being made in radiometric calculations. Indeed, he captions a picture of a moon rock with the words 'Radioactive dating shows it is 4500 million years old, the same age as the Earth.'

It will be worth analysing in detail how Johnson presents this information to students. The following quote is a worked example from his text book.

In a rock sample, the proportion of ^{238}U atoms to ^{206}Pb atoms was found to be 4:1. How old is the rock?

This means that, on average, for every 5 atoms of ^{238}U when the rock was formed, 1 atom has decayed and 4 atoms have not decayed yet. That is, $\frac{4}{5}$ atoms are still radioactive ^{238}U.[8]

This is not good teaching, because a number of presuppositions have not been presented to the students. No good teacher of physics, whether evolutionist or creationist, would object to such a numerical calculation being undertaken, especially as it involves reading a graph. Nevertheless, the student should be informed of the presuppositions used in the calculation. It is noteworthy that Johnson is leading the students to suppose that all of the lead-206 atoms came originally from uranium-238—that is, it is assumed that the rock contained no lead-206 at its formation. Students should be encouraged to challenge this presupposition.

The example continues:

So the activity is 80% of the initial activity. From the half-life graph for ^{238}U we find that this has taken about 1500 million years.

Other radio-isotopes are sometimes used. ^{235}U (half-life = 700 million years) also decays to Lead. Potassium-40 decays to Argon-40 with a half-life of 1400 million years.

The graph has not been produced from measured data. It has been produced from calculated data, based on an assumption that the half-life of uranium-238 has not changed. One group of creation scientists—the so-called RATE group (Radioactivity and the Age of The Earth)—have found compelling evidence that the rate of decay of such isotopes has not been constant.[9]

After this final extract from the worked example, which is actually just a statement of further opinions, Johnson ought to have pointed out that different radio-isotopes often give wildly different results. A fair appraisal of radiometric dating ought also to point out that rocks of known age (e.g. from volcanic eruptions) sometimes present apparent radiometric ages of millions of years. Examples of both these can be found in the RATE books referred to above, or in the somewhat easier to understand summary work, *Thousands not Billions*.[10]

Turning now to the way that examination syllabuses interpret Sc4.4d, we find that the OCR syllabus records four statements as being derived from NC Sc4.4d. These are as follows:

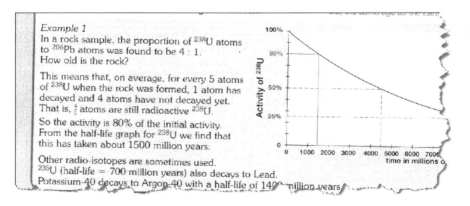

Example 1
In a rock sample, the proportion of ^{238}U atoms to ^{206}Pb atoms was found to be 4 : 1.
How old is the rock?

This means that, on average, for every 5 atoms of ^{238}U when the rock was formed, 1 atom has decayed and 4 atoms have not decayed yet. That is, $\frac{4}{5}$ atoms are still radioactive ^{238}U.

So the activity is 80% of the initial activity. From the half-life graph for ^{238}U we find that this has taken about 1500 million years.

Other radio-isotopes are sometimes used. ^{235}U (half-life = 700 million years) also decays to Lead. Potassium-40 decays to Argon-40 with a half-life of 1400 million years.

Candidates should be able to:

- (OCR4.7.9) Explain that theories for the origin of the Universe must take into account that:
  - ○ Light from other galaxies is shifted to the red end of the spectrum
  - ○ The further away galaxies are, the greater the red shift
- (OCR4.7.10) Recognise that one way of explaining this is that:
  - ○ Other galaxies are moving away from us very quickly
  - ○ Galaxies furthest from us are moving fastest
- (OCR4.7.11) Explain how knowledge of the rate of expansion of the Universe enables its age to be estimated
- (OCR4.7.12) Explain that there are possible futures for the Universe depending on the amount of mass in the Universe and the speed at which the galaxies are moving apart.[11]

Interestingly, the OCR syllabus follows these statements up with another statement, linked to NC Sci.1b—that 'pupils should be taught how scientific controversies can arise from different ways of interpreting empirical evidence.

Candidates should be able to:

- (OCR4.7.13) interpret given information about developments in ideas on the origin of the Universe.[12]

This latter statement is to be applauded, and should enable much imaginative teaching of how worldviews affect interpretation. It gives the teacher the opportunity to encourage students to challenge presuppositions.

Statement OCR4.7.9 above is advocating that students should be taught an appreciation of factual observations. Big Bang theory attempts to take red shift measurements into account, as do creationist cosmologies, such as those discussed by Humphreys[13] and Williams and Hartnett.[14] OCR4.7.10 then suggests the teaching of 'one way of explaining' the origin of the universe. Helpfully, the explanation given is not exclusive.

As a slight digression from the subject at hand, it is noted that GCSE physics is frequently taught in comprehensive schools in England and Wales by non-physicists, due to the shortage of physics graduates prepared to take a career in teaching. Statement OCR4.7.10 is ambiguous, and could be used by non-specialist physics teachers, who perhaps would not understand cosmology too well themselves, to describe a three-dimensional material universe expanding into an empty, physical, three-dimensional cosmos. Such an image is a common misconception, yet does not form part of either Big Bang or creationist cosmologies. Most cosmologies instead maintain that the galaxies are not moving apart from each other by very much with respect to space itself, but that space itself is expanding. This is in accord with many passages in Scripture, which describe God as the One 'who created the heavens and stretched them out' (Isaiah 42:5).

In statement OCR4.7.11, the writers of the syllabus allow facts to be confused with their presuppositions. They assume that the universe's rate of expansion is constant—an unwarranted assumption. They therefore lead students to believe that traditional Big Bang calculations of the age of the universe are factual, rather than suppositional. This statement allows for only one idea about the origin of the universe, and is therefore not in line with the NC statement Sc4.4d.

Statement OCR4.7.12 goes beyond the remit of a science syllabus, making an unscientific statement about futures of the Universe. It is not possible for scientists to look into such matters, and the proposed 'heat death' of the Universe is in direct opposition to the teachings of the Bible.

The WJEC syllabus takes Big Bang and evolutionary presuppositions much further than the OCR syllabus. The WJEC requires the following to be taught about the origins of stars.

state that stars, including our Sun, form when dust and gas from space is pulled together by gravitational attraction and that their life time is finite.[15]

Evolutionary astrophysicists point out that there is no current workable Big Bang model of how stars actually formed, so this statement is unscientific.

The big bang theory can boast of no quantitative predictions that have subsequently been validated by observation. The successes claimed by the theory's supporters consist of its ability to retrospectively fit observations with a steadily increasing array of adjustable parameters, just as the old Earth-centered cosmology of Ptolemy needed layer upon layer of epicycles.[16]

The WJEC then gives very detailed expansions of the NC statements, which fail to take any ideas other than the Big Bang into account.

state that stars are very massive so that the force of gravity drawing together the matter from which they are made is very strong. The very high temperatures in stars create forces acting in the opposite direction. During the stable period of the life of a star, these forces are balanced. The Sun is at this stage in its life

state that, thereafter, the star then expands to become a red giant. At a later stage in its history it contracts under its own gravity to become a white dwarf. The matter from which the star is made may then be millions of times denser than any matter on Earth. If the star is massive enough, it may then explode throwing dust and gas into space. A very dense neutron star or black hole could remain;[17]

The first of these statements presupposes that scientists know exactly what forces are at play within a star. They do not. The second statement presupposes that the life-cycle of stars is known. It is not, as it has not been observed. The traditional star life-cycle is inferred by means of Big Bang cosmologies which are not even accepted by all secular astrophysicists.

After 'red shift' statements, almost identical to the OCR, the WJEC then goes on to require that candidates should:

know that the faster a galaxy is moving, the greater is the shift towards the red end of the spectrum;[18]

Once again, a syllabus is erroneously attributing red shift to movement of galaxies, rather than expansion of space.

understand how these ideas support a model of an expanding universe which originated approximately 12 billion years ago with the 'BIG BANG'.[19]

This is poor science. Students are being instructed that 'ideas support ... the BIG BANG', when it is known that an increasing number of secular astrophysicists do not accept the Big Bang. To claim that observations definitely support Big Bang cosmology, therefore, is an error.

In his text book, Johnson seems to make a slightly better job than the syllabuses at explaining spatial expansion. He uses the common illustration of an inflating balloon.

> This means that the whole Universe is expanding, just like the dots on a balloon move further apart as the balloon expands.[20]

Although the analogy makes sense, Johnson does not explain that the galaxies, represented by the dots, are not moving apart with respect to the fabric of the balloon, but are 'pushed' further apart by the expansion of the balloon.

Johnson also confuses fact with presupposition.

> By measuring the rate of expansion of the Universe as it is now, astronomers can calculate that the Big Bang was about 12,000 million years ago [21]

In one sentence, Johnson has assumed that the rate of expansion can be measured accurately, that the rate of expansion has always been constant, and that the Big Bang actually happened. That is three presuppositions in one short sentence, yet his readers are presented with this information as 'fact'. Indeed, on the same page Johnson goes on to present models of the universe that actually *require* changes in the rate of expansion.

In these examples, we have seen that current teaching of GCSE physics is requiring presuppositions to be taught to children as if they were facts. Johnson and the OCR come together to commit one final inadvertent deception on their students, as Johnson uses a former OCR exam question, thus:

a. What is meant by red shift?
b. What is a light year?

c. A galaxy is 1200 million light years away from us. It is moving away from us at 30,000 km/s, which is one-tenth (0.1) of the speed of light. Assuming that its speed has been constant and that all the matter in the Universe was originally in one place, how long has it taken for the galaxy and us to be this far apart?

d. *What is the significance of this value?* (emphasis mine)[22]

Questions a. and b. are non-controversial. Question c. involves presuppositions, but at least the presuppositions are actually explicitly stated. The calculation is as follows:

$$s = v.t$$
(where s is distance, v is velocity and t is time)
$$\therefore t = s / v$$
$$\therefore t = 1200 \text{ million} / 0.1$$
$$\therefore t = 12{,}000 \text{ million years}$$

The calculation is pretty straightforward, and should not tax most students (though, as a former schoolteacher, I know that many candidates would struggle with such a calculation). However, question d. asks for the significance of the number. The significance that the students are expected to offer is that the number is the age of the universe, according to Big Bang cosmology. Such an answer is rather disingenuous. It allows children to think that they have independently calculated the age of the universe, when, in fact, the original figures given were chosen deliberately to give the answer required. There is a *hidden curriculum* behind such questions, and our children are being misled.

Chemistry

There is little of concern in chemistry, other than that its National Curriculum euphemism—'Materials and their properties'—enables it to take in aspects of Earth science. A small number of points may be of concern, however.

Pupils should be taught:
Sc3.2p How the Earth's atmosphere and oceans have changed over time

Sc3.2r How the sequence of, and evidence for, rock formation and deformation is obtained from the rock record[23]

The Welsh curriculum contains the following:

Pupils should be taught:
Sc3.2.22 How the atmosphere and oceans evolved to their present composition
Sc3.2.24 How plate tectonic processes are involved in the formation, deformation and recycling of rocks
Sc3.2.25 How the sequence of, and evidence for, these processes is obtained from the rock record.[24]

Statement Sc3.2r could be used to include Huttonian or Lyellian geological ages. On the other hand, it could equally be used to aid qualitative analysis of *in situ* weathering. Statement Sc3.2p contains the presupposition that the Earth's atmosphere and oceans have indeed changed over time. It is possible that this point could be used to back up evolutionary theory by proposing the unlikely 'primeval soup' used to explain chemical evolution.

The Welsh curriculum is more blatantly evolutionary than that of England in these examples. Sc3.2.22 actually uses the word 'evolve'. Also, Welsh children are required to know something about plate tectonics, a topic not covered in the English NC Core.

As with our analysis of physics, we will consider the implications of these NC statements to the OCR and WJEC science syllabuses.

The OCR syllabus expands Sc3.2p into no fewer than *nine* statements, lending the statement an importance beyond traditional chemical teaching on the Periodic Table or the atomic model. The nine statements will be quoted, sometimes in groups, and then addressed.

Candidates should be able to:
- (OCR 3.7.1) recall that the present atmosphere:
  - Has been much the same for the past 200 million years
  - Consists, for dry air, of approximately four fifths nitrogen, one fifth oxygen with other gases including the noble gases and carbon dioxide[25]

The second bullet of OCR3.7.1 is uncontroversial, and can even be demonstrated experimentally in the lab. The experiment that I used to perform, involving the ignition of red phosphorus in a bell jar, partially immersed in water, is now considered too dangerous, and is one of the many practical demonstrations of chemistry, remembered from my childhood, now denied to modern chemistry students. The partially submerged bell jar trapped air, and the height of the trapped air can be measured. Inside the jar, a small glass dish contains red phosphorous. When this is ignited, it burns. Phosphorus combines with the oxygen in the trapped air, forming fumes of phosphorous pentoxide. Phosphorous pentoxide is soluble in water, so the products do not take up space. The oxygen has been removed from the trapped air to form this oxide, so the water level inside the bell jar rises, to replace the removed oxygen. The new height of the air inside the jar is found to be about four fifths of the original height, showing that oxygen comprises about one fifth of the mixture of gases in the air.

The first bullet of the statement is notable in that it acknowledges the lack of change in atmospheric composition. However, it contains a statement of deep time which is presuppositional not factual.

- (OCR3.7.2) describe a simple experiment, using gas syringes, to show that air contains approximately one fifth oxygen by volume
- (OCR3.7.3) recall that one currently held view is that the Earth's first atmosphere was formed by intense volcanic activity and probably consisted of carbon dioxide and water vapour with smaller amounts of ammonia and methane

The much more tame demonstration required in this syllabus involves pushing air, using graduated gas syringes, over a heated tube, containing an excess of copper granules. The copper reacts, extremely tamely, with oxygen in the air. Once the hot air has cooled down, the gas syringe, previously measuring 100cm^3, will show 79cm^3, illustrating that 21cm^3 has now been removed—the 21cm^3 being oxygen that had reacted with the copper to form copper oxide. As this is a teacher demonstration, if the syringe doesn't show the 'right' amount, it is always possible to push or pull it a bit to give the 'correct' value Readers might be shocked to know how often such techniques are used by teachers, invalidating the observational value of many educational scientific experiments.

OCR 3.7.3 is much more problematic. At least the statement acknowledges that the primeval atmosphere theory is only 'one currently held view'. Nevertheless, the use of the word 'probably' lends an authenticity to what is, in fact, a case of putting the cart before the horse.

The only reason for proposing this unusual reducing atmosphere early in the Earth's history is because evolutionists want to find a way of producing organic molecules prior to the supposed evolution of life. It is an oblique reference back to the old, now discredited, Miller-Urey experiment.

The classic experiment was carried out in 1953 by graduate student, Stanley Miller, and his advisor, Harold Urey. The mixture of gases used was similar to the suggestions of OCR 3.7.3 above, but with the notable addition of hydrogen. Miller heated water in this gaseous mixture, in a glass apparatus from which all air had been previously removed. These gases were circulated by pump, past a high-voltage electric spark. This is because of the hypothesis of the time that suggested life could have begun in such a primordial soup under the action of flashes of lightning. After the experiment had been conducted for a week, Miller analysed the resulting compounds that had been formed and found many of them to be amino acids, which are the building blocks of proteins, which in turn are necessary for life. Hence the experiment was hailed as the formation of life in the laboratory.

In a discussion of the Miller-Urey experiment, Wells has drawn attention to a number of problems.[26]

Amino acids are complex organic molecules. All but the simplest can exist in at least two forms, which are mirror images of each other. This is due to the fact that carbon atoms bond tetrahedrally to four other groups. If all four groups are different, then two mirror images exist. An analogy for these mirror-image molecules is to consider our hands, which look the same. They are in fact 'mirror images'. Try putting your right hand exactly over the top of your left hand and you will see that they do not coincide.

When such mirror images exist, they have exactly the same chemical properties and most of the same physical properties. However, they have the odd property that they rotate plane-polarised light which might be shone through solutions of the amino acids. The two mirror images rotate the plane-polarised light by the same angle, but one rotates to the left and the other to the right.

The Miller-Urey experiment produces, as one might expect, a 50:50 mixture of the two *optical isomers*. However, proteins in living organisms contain only the 'left-handed' version. Production of a single optical isomer does not seem possible by simple chemical methods in the manner of the Miller-Urey experiment.

Another problem with the Miller-Urey experiment is the choice of gases for this supposed primeval atmosphere. The reason for the choice is two-fold. Firstly, because it is clear that such gases might be precursors of amino acids, and secondly, because the presence of oxygen molecules, which often behave as if they were free radicals, would immediately destroy any complex organic molecule with which it came into contact.

The 'primeval atmosphere' scenario presupposes that oxygen would be produced later in the organic chemical evolution by photosynthesis of carbon dioxide. This, it is presumed, would reduce the level of CO_2. However, oxygen would have been formed almost immediately by *photo*

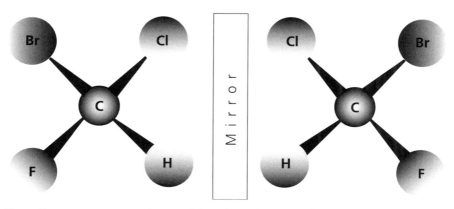

Enantioners, non-superimposable mirror images of fluorochlorobromomethane, CHClFBr

dissociation of water molecules. Wells shows that there would have been sufficient oxygen produced by this method to completely ruin the chemical evolution process.

These and other problems associated with the primeval atmosphere model are at least recognised by the OCR syllabus with its emphasis that this is only one current model. However, it can be seen that the subsequent syllabus statements build on statement OCR 3.7.3 as if it were factual.

- (OCR 3.7.4) explain how the evolution of photosynthesising organisms on land and in the sea resulted in an increase in the amount of oxygen
- (OCR 3.7.5) describe how the reduction in the amount of carbon dioxide in the atmosphere was mainly due to
  ○ It dissolving in the oceans, much of this then forming sedimentary rocks
  ○ Its removal by photosynthesis
  ○ The formation of fossil fuels
- (OCR 3.7.6) recall that ammonia in the early atmosphere was removed by:
  ○ Nitrifying bacteria, which changed the ammonia into nitrates
  ○ Conversion into nitrogen by denitrifying bacteria
  ○ Reaction with oxygen

All of the above statements follow only from a presupposition that the Earth once had a primeval reducing atmosphere, rather than the present oxidising atmosphere.

(OCR 3.7.7) recall that the oceans were formed by condensation of the water vapour in the primitive atmosphere as the Earth cooled

This statement uses a previously unannounced presupposition—that the Earth cooled down from a gaseous state. The astronomical model required to furnish such a presupposition—not covered in the physics section of the syllabus—is itself fraught with unresolved difficulties.

- (OCR 3.7.8) describe how the composition of the oceans has evolved over millions of years and that it depends on the balance between the:
  ○ Input of dissolved salts from the weathering of rocks

○ Removal of dissolved salts by shell formation in marine organisms
○ Chemical reactions to form sea-floor sediments and crystallisation to form salt deposits

OCR 3.7.8 does not give strong support to chemical evolutionists. The rate at which salt is input to oceans is much greater than the rate of salt removal, so there is an overall salt input. If the oceans began as distilled water, it can be shown that the present level of salt concentration could not have taken longer than 12 million years. This figure is far too small for evolutionists. It must be emphasised that this calculation of 12 million years is an upper limit. I am not saying that I believe the world to be 12 million years old. Creationists are happy that such results are consistent with an age for the Earth of 6000 years, because it is unlikely that the oceans were created as pure, distilled water, and the events of the Flood would have seriously affected the concentration of salts.[27]

The remaining statement is:

● (OCR 3.7.9) explain the importance of the oceans as a gas reservoir for carbon dioxide

This statement is uncontroversial, and is verifiable by experiment.

The WJEC syllabus is less easy to reference, and contains similar statements, but also contains some classic presuppositions masquerading as facts.

Candidates should: know that oxygen originally appeared as a 'polluting' gas and is entirely biological in origin.[28]

There is absolutely no evidence to show that oxygen is 'entirely biological in origin', or that it appeared as a polluting gas by outgassing from volcanoes. Such a position is not even believed by all evolutionary scientists.

Returning to the NC statements, the OCR syllabus divides statement Sc3.2r into four statements. Three of these statements are uncontroversial, because they make no statements about time or supposition, encouraging only observation and the honest application of plate tectonic theory. However, one of the OCR's statements has a good deal of baggage.

- (OCR 3.7.12) explain how the sequence of rock formation can be obtained from the rock record:
  - ○ A rock higher in a sequence is usually younger than one below it
  - ○ A rock which cuts across another is younger
  - ○ How fossil evidence helps to date rocks[29]

The first two bullet points are interpretive statements which may or may not be correct. Given that there might be something in the suggestions, science teachers ought to point out that the order is frequently reversed.

The third bullet point is a big giveaway. Most rocks are not dated by radiometric methods. Most rocks are dated by the *index* fossils contained within them. These are fossils of creatures said to have lived only in a limited era. This is clearly a presupposition.

It should also be noted that many index fossils are dated according to the rocks in which they are found Because fossils are used to date layers, evolutionists can then point to fossils in an upper layer and state that they evolved later, so it confirms that the rock on top came later. Thus they 'prove' what they assumed to be true in the first place

The WJEC syllabus contains a lot more geology, reflecting the greater importance of Earth science in the Welsh National Curriculum. The WJEC syllabus contains a whole section on Geological Processes. Most of this is good science, referring only to ages as 'relative ages', determined by observation. One statement stands out, however, and it is the first of the geological statements.

Understand that sedimentary rocks, such as limestone and sandstone, are formed from layers of sediment and that the increased pressure, caused by burial under further layers of sediment, expels water or air and compacts the sediments together, the process often taking place over millions of years.[30]

Many scientists have shown[31] that sedimentation can be rapid. Thus, the syllabus writers once again have allowed themselves to be influenced by their own presuppositions.

In chemistry, as in physics, children are being taught presupposition as if it were fact. Once again, they are being misled.

Biology

It is in the area of biology that one might have thought there would be ample opportunity for evolutionary presuppositions to influence the curriculum. Surprisingly, there are fewer definite evolutionary presuppositions in the National Curriculum in the Biology Attainment Target than one might expect, when compared with chemistry or physics.

Only two NC statements in the English Curriculum cause concern and these are clearly labelled as 'evolution'.

Sc2.4i that the fossil record is evidence for evolution
Sc2.4j how variation and selection may lead to evolution or to extinction[32]

The National Curriculum in Wales has identical wording for these two points, and they are found at Sc2.4.9 and Sc2.4.10.[33]

Statement Sc2.4i has already been addressed in section 8.3, 'The Use of Fossils'. Sc2.4i is not an example of scientism—it is simply a demonstrably incorrect statement.

Statement Sc2.4j should not cause concern if taught correctly. Creationists accept variation and natural selection. New species arise within the created kinds, or 'baramins'. Creationists' problem with the statement is the inclusion of the word 'evolution'. If this were changed to 'speciation' or simply 'development of new species', there would be no difficulty. The presupposition involved in this statement is the original Darwinian fallacy—the fallacy that changes and speciation in a population of finches, for example, is to be equated with molecules-to-man evolution. Some creationists get around this issue by attempting to distinguish between *microevolution*, which they define as variation within a baramin, and *macroevolution*, which they define as the erroneous concept of molecules-to-man evolution. Answers in Genesis[34] prefers not to use the terms micro and macro-evolution, as evolution always implies, in our opinion, an increase in genetic information. Such an increase in genetic information is not observed. We prefer to refer to macroevolution as simply evolution—we may sometimes explain it as molecules-to-man evolution. The so-called microevolution we would not refer to as evolution at all—preferring to call it variation, or speciation, or a similar term. It is not the size of the change that is important ('micro-' or 'macro-') but the direction of change. Change that requires an increase in genetic information does not happen.

Looking at how the syllabuses treat Sc2.4i, the OCR seem to have worded their statement slightly more fairly that the NC, though their presupposition is still evident.

● (OCR2.10.23) explain briefly how organisms may have become fossilised and recognise that fossils provide evidence for evolution[35]

The word 'briefly' helps teachers give an idea of the importance (or rather, lack of importance) to stress for this statement. Also, the word 'may' is helpful in this context. Although the second clause of the statement is still from an evolutionary presupposition, it seems slightly preferable to say 'fossils provide evidence' rather than 'the fossil record is evidence'. The NC statement is definite, whereas the OCR statement is open to interpretation.

The WJEC is more biased on this issue than the OCR.

Know that organisms have changed over time/evolution and fossils provide evidence for these changes. Fossils are the 'remains' of plants or animals from many years ago which are found in rocks. *The study of fossils from different aged rocks show changes in form over time*. Species may become extinct if the environment changes [emphasis mine].[36]

It has already been shown above that the statement in italics does not accord with the evidence.

The syllabuses cause more problems with their interpretations of Sc2.4j. The OCR uses two statements:

● (OCR2.10.21) explain the meaning of Darwin's four observations that lead to his theory of evolution

○ All organisms potentially over reproduce
○ Population numbers tend to remain fairly constant over long periods of time
○ Organisms demonstrate variation
○ Some of the variations are inherited
● (OCR2.10.22) describe how the process of natural selection may result in:
○ Changes within a species, as illustrated by the peppered moth
○ Many changes over a period of time which may lead to a new species
○ Failure of a species to change which may lead to extinction[37]

OCR2.10.21 is implying that the four observations lead inevitably to accepting evolution. However, such acceptance is not inevitable, from Darwin's observations. There is nothing that creationists would disagree with in statement OCR2.10.22, apart from pointing out that the peppered moth experiment was fraudulent, as mentioned in section 8.2 above. It is likely that evolutionists would use the second bullet point to emphasise evolution, but speciation is not evolution, as we have seen in section 8.2.

The greater detail in the WJEC syllabus once again leads to more bias.

When provided with appropriate information, distinguish between the theories of Darwin and Lamarck and suggest reasons for the different theories, and suggest reasons why Darwin's theory was not readily accepted.[38]

It is actually probably quite helpful to compel teachers to distinguish between Darwin and Lamarck, as many inexperienced or non-specialist teachers of biology frequently confuse their theories. An additional advantage is to give the lie to the idea that creation was the only alternative to Darwinism, when, in fact, other evolutionary ideas had often been preferred to the biblical account. Mortenson has shown in great detail how Darwin's ideas were accepted early by theologians, because of theological liberalism.[39]

The WJEC syllabus continues:

Understand that all the species which exist today have evolved, via mutation and natural selection, from simple life-forms which first developed more than three billion years ago.

The above statement is completely unjustified by the NC, and is a blatant statement of evolutionary bias and presupposition. A teacher teaching this statement as fact would be guilty of teaching falsehoods—although many of them would be doing so unawares. Perhaps it becomes more understandable, however, when the next WJEC statement is read, showing a degree of what can only be described as ignorance.

Understand that evolution of resistant bacteria can result from the over use of antibiotics

It is undeniable that some bacteria become resistant to antibiotics. However, this is not evolution, because it is not caused by increase in genetic information. It is not difficult to understand how antibiotic resistance comes about. Carl Wieland, formerly a medical doctor, explains it thus:

Notice that:

i. This is why multiple resistance to major antibiotics is more common in hospitals which treat more serious conditions—these are the hospitals which will frequently be using the sophisticated, expensive 'heavy artillery' antibiotics, so this sort of 'natural selection' will happen more often.

ii. In this kind of instance, the information to resist the antibiotic was already there in the bacterial population—it did not arise by itself, or in response to the antibiotic.[40]

In the same article, Dr Wieland shows that antibiotic resistance can also arise by mutations, but these mutations always involve loss of genetic information, not gain. The 'beneficial' mutation of the bacteria is fine in a hospital environment, where there are so few bacteria around. The mutation, however, causes defects in other ways in the bacteria. The 'advantage' of their mutation is similar to the advantage experienced by eyeless fish in dark caves—they will not get infections, due to accidental injury, of their eyes. There have been scientists who have suggested that such fish have 'evolved the ability to be blind', but few scientists would really see such loss of genetic information as evolution.

The way that a biology text book has interpreted some of the syllabus statements above has already been analysed. It can be noted, in conclusion, that in biology, as in chemistry and physics, children are being deliberately taught untruths. However, biology is not more guilty of this misinformation than the other two sciences. The reason for this misinformation is that the writers of the National Curriculum documents, syllabuses and text books are bound by presuppositions which they allow to guide their writings as if they were facts. These presuppositions are often not recognised by ordinary science teachers. They form part of a secular philosophy which underpins modern science education. This philosophy is not itself part of science. It is akin to a religious belief. Evolutionist Professor Hiram Caton showed that he understood this fact when he said:

The long evolutionary past removes the Judaeo-Christian God to an infinite distance and finally extinguishes Him in the belief that our species is the chance product of blind natural forces. We are on our own and consequently we may do what we will, free of ancient prohibitions and divinely-sanctioned codes. This liberation doctrine (evolution) is the basis of the most audacious politics ever attempted—the control of human evolution—and it is a salvation doctrine rivalling the Gospel.[41]

Evolutionists should not pretend that National Curriculum Science is a neutral subject. It is value-laden with philosophy and religion, with faith in the god of scientism.

Notes

1 See, for example, **E. J. Lerner,** 'Bucking the Big Bang', *New Scientist:* 22 May 2004, p. 20.
2 Ibid.
3 See **A. Williams** and **J. Hartnett,** *Dismantling the Big Bang* (Green Forest, AR: Master Books, 2005).
4 Commentary from **Richard Dawkins** TV documentary *The Root of all Evil?* This question was from part one, 'The God Delusion', broadcast on the UK's Channel 4 network on Monday 9 January 2006.
5 Science: The National Curriculum for England, QCA: 1999, p. 56.
6 Science in the National Curriculum in Wales, ACCAC: 2000, p. 55.
7 **K. Johnson,** *Physics for you* (Nelson Thornes, 2001), p. 362.

8 Ibid. p. 362.

9 L. Vardiman, et al, *Radioisotopes and the Age of The Earth* (ICR/CRS: 2000).

10 D. DeYoung, *Thousands not Billions* (Green Forest, AR: Master Books: 2005).

11 OCR GCSE Double Award Linear Science, 2001, p. 67.

12 Ibid. p. 67.

13 R. Humphreys, *Starlight and Time* (Green Forest, AR: Master Books, 1994).

14 A. Williams and **J. Hartnett,** *Dismantling the Big Bang* (Green Forest, AR: Master Books, 2005).

15 GCSE Science: Double Award (A), (Welsh Joint Education Committee: 2000), p. 59.

16 E. J. Lerner, *et al, An Open Letter to the Scientific Community*, New Scientist, 22 May, 2004, also found at http://www.cosmologystatement.org.

17 Ibid. p. 60.

18 Ibid.

19 Ibid.

20 K. Johnson, op. cit., p. 166.

21 Ibid, p. 166.

22 Ibid, p. 173.

23 Science: The National Curriculum for England, QCA: 1999, p. 52.

24 Science in the National Curriculum in Wales, ACCAC: 2000, p. 50.

25 This statement, and the quotation of the next eight syllabus statements, are all taken from OCR GCSE Double Award Linear Science, 2001, p. 54.

26 J. Wells, *Icons of Evolution* (New York: Regnery, 2000), pp. 9–27.

27 D.R. Humphreys, *Evidence for a Young World* (Petersburg, KY: Answers in Genesis), p. 8.

28 GCSE Science: Double Award (A), (Welsh Joint Education Committee:2000), p. 42.

29 OCR syllabus, p. 55.

30 WJEC syllabus, p. 40.

31 REFERENCE Guy Berthault.

32 Science: The National Curriculum for England, QCA: 1999, p. 50.

33 Science in the National Curriculum in Wales, ACCAC: 2000, p. 49.

34 Answers in Genesis is the ministry for which I work, as speaker and writer. See the Introduction to this book or see the website, www.answersingenesis.org

35 OCR GCSE Double Award Linear Science, 2001, p. 41.

36 GCSE Science: Double Award (A), (Welsh Joint Education Committee, 2000), p. 24.

37 OCR syllabus, p. 41.

38 This, and the following few quotations, are from WJEC syllabus, pp. 24–25.

39 T. Mortenson, *The Great Turning Point*, Master Books, 2004.

40 C. Wieland, 'Superbugs: not super after all', *Creation,* **10**(1), 10–13.
41 H. Caton, *Quadrant,* May 1987, p. 68.

Chapter 10

Scientism's influence in non-science curriculum areas

O ne of the most surprising and disturbing elements in education is how the presuppositions of scientism are beginning to make their mark in other curriculum areas outside science.

We observed in section 3.2 ('The Spiritual Dimension of Science in the National Curriculum') that British schools can often be seen as assembly lines. Such an approach would be alien to many primary schools where all curriculum areas are often delivered through cross-curricular themes. This is one of the reasons many pupils can suffer a culture shock when they transfer from one type of school to another, usually at the age of eleven.

The Science National Curriculum strongly recommends linkages to other curriculum areas, and communicates these, with clear references to the NC statements. The Science NC in England suggests links to English, Mathematics, and Information and Communications Technology (ICT). The Science NC in Wales mentions all of these, as well as links to Personal, Social, Citizenship and Health Education (PSCHE) and the Curriculum Cymreig, a rather vague concept, which suggests that, where possible, teaching examples should be drawn from Welsh life, geography and culture.

For example, the Science NC in Wales has a statement at Sc2.5.4, in Key Stage 3 which states:

Pupils should be taught … about the ways in which living things and the environment of Wales can be protected and the importance of conserving biodiversity.[1]

The documentation suggests that the teaching of this statement could be linked to PSCHE and to the Curriculum Cymreig. In Key Stage 4, statement Sc1.2.3 says:

… to work quantitatively to an appropriate degree of precision, using mathematical conventions and units appropriate to their work.[2]

This is obviously linked to the Mathematics NC.

The links in the Science NC documents for England are more specific. For example, statement Sc2.3b states:

Pupils should be taught ... that the rate of photosynthesis may be limited by light intensity, carbon dioxide concentration or temperature[3]

The document clearly links this to the Mathematics statement Ma4.5c.

Students should be taught to ... look at data to find patterns and exceptions.[4]

Although explicit references in the other National Curriculum documents to Science are rarer, it is still considered good practice for such linkages to be made.

Links with Religious Education

The subject Religious Education holds a unique place in the state school curriculum of England and Wales. Under the 1944 Education Act, Religious Studies, or Religious Education, was a compulsory subject. Indeed, it was the only compulsory subject in that Act. The statutory nature of RE was reaffirmed in the 1988 act, which introduced the National Curriculum, and was again reaffirmed in the Acts of 1996 and 1998. Thus RE is a statutory, compulsory subject, though not part of the National Curriculum.

It must be remembered—particularly in view of the fact that this section is going to quote from a Scottish syllabus—that the law concerning education in Scotland is different from that of England or Wales, and education legislation for Scotland is now the responsibility of the devolved Scottish Parliament. The subject in Scotland, which is also compulsory, is known as Religious and Moral Education (RME).

Because RE in England and Wales is not a National Curriculum subject, there is no compulsory syllabus. Instead, the syllabuses are devised locally by committees known as SACRE—Standing Advisory Council on Religious Education. Every Local Education Authority (LEA) is required to have a SACRE by law. A SACRE contains representatives from RE teachers, local religious leaders and council members. The 'Christian' representative is usually a vicar from the Church of England. If he/she is liberal in theology, then there will almost certainly be no biblical Christian input to that committee. In Wales, SACREs usually have representatives of the Anglican Church in Wales, despite the fact that Wales has no established denomination, unlike England.

Consequently, there is no national standard syllabus for RE. However, the website of the Department for Education and Skills (DfES) has a sample syllabus, given as an example of good practice. This sample RE syllabus contains some items of interest to this study.[5] The referenced portion is for Key Stage 3 pupils (ages 11 to 14) to study 'Where did the universe come from?' This particular unit has some helpful background pointers, under the heading 'Expectations'. Two statements from this section are given below:

Most pupils will know that a person's world-view shapes and is shaped by their scientific and religious beliefs.

Some pupils … will … describe key beliefs and teachings about creation and evolution.[6]

However, after that excellent start, we soon see evolutionary or non-biblical presuppositions creeping into the scheme of work.

Pupils should … explain the nature and meanings of the Genesis creation stories for theists, creationists and others.[7]

This passage presupposes that there is more than one creation story in Genesis. It is the old chestnut that Genesis 1 and 2 are differing accounts. In fact, they are not. Genesis 2 is simply an expansion of the account of the creation of mankind. Yet there is no acknowledgement in the sample syllabus that the unity of Genesis 1 and 2 is even a valid interpretation. The outworking of this point of view is seen further in the following extract:

Pupils should ... read, discuss and analyse Genesis 1–3, looking at the different strands of the material, *e.g. P and J*, and its literary genres, *e.g. poetry, myth*.[8]

Two presuppositions are being presented to the pupils in this extract. The 'literary strands' P and J refer to the 'Documentary Hypothesis'. This is the view that Genesis was actually compiled from an intertwining of earlier (conveniently lost) documents, called J, E, D and P. The belief is that Genesis 1–3 were compiled from the J, or Jahwist strand, and the P or Priestly strand. Russell Grigg has this to say about the Documentary Hypothesis.

Ultimately, the author of Genesis was God, working through Moses. This does not mean that God used Moses as a 'typewriter'. Rather, God prepared Moses for his task from the day he was born. When the time came, Moses had all the necessary data, and was infallibly guided by the Holy Spirit as to what he included and what he left out. This is consistent with known history and with the claims and principles of Scripture (2 Timothy 3:15–17; 2 Peter 1:20–21).

On the other hand there is no historical evidence, and no spiritual or theological basis whatsoever for the deceptive JEDP hypothesis. Its teaching is completely false; the 'scholarship' that promotes it is totally spurious. Propped up by the theory of evolution, it exists solely to undermine the authority of the Word of God.[9]

Another presupposition is that parts of Genesis 1–3 could be poetry or myth. Either of these labels enables the viewpoint to be expressed that Genesis is not *literally* true, but is true in some *symbolic* or *spiritual* sense. Yet the literary style of Genesis 1–3 is the same as that of the rest of Genesis—it is written as if it were actual history. It is therefore completely consistent for us to claim that Genesis 1–3 is indeed actual history.

One wonders if the writers of this sample RE syllabus are aware of the lack of credibility attached to the theory which it is recommending to its students.

Scottish RMPS Higher

The Scottish education system examines school students at two levels—standard grade and higher grade. These are approximately equivalent to GCSEs and A-levels in England and Wales.

The following example is taken from the Religious, Moral and Philosophical Studies Higher syllabus. In a unit of study entitled 'Christianity: Belief and Science', students are encouraged to see the differences between different worldviews and their approaches to science. However, the definition used of these viewpoints in the syllabus is erroneous, and, one has to say, biased. The syllabus defines three possible relationships between science and Christianity.

Relationship 1: the rejection of scientific enquiry as a reliable source of understanding.

Relationship 2: the rejection of revelation as a reliable source of understanding.

Relationship 3: the acceptance of both revelation and scientific enquiry as reliable sources of understanding.[10]

Relationship 1 is then clearly equated with creationism.[11]

I have been in correspondence with concerned Scottish school teachers, but at the time of writing, the SQA have refused all requests to reword these definitions. This would seem to be a very clear example of presuppositional bias in favour of evolutionary propaganda.

A musical example

One of the most shocking examples of the introduction of scientism to other subjects that we have seen is in a music book. The National Curriculum document for music is not at fault: the lesson we are about to analyse refers to section Mu 4b of the NC.[12] In this section, pupils are to be taught such changes in musical notes as *pitch*.

A.C. Black is a major publisher of good educational materials. Their otherwise excellent book, *Music Express: Year 2* contains a section using Saint-Saëns' piece 'Fossils', taken from his suite, *Carnival of the Animals*.[13] It is often useful for small children to learn rhythms by chanting words. Year 2 children are aged six to seven years old.

In order to learn the rhythms and pitch of *Fossils*, the children use this verse:

Fossils in the rock
Pterydactyl (*sic*) teeth
Millions of years made an ammonite

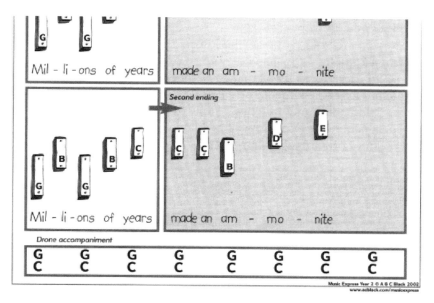

It is perfectly possible that the book's author does not fully appreciate the controversy over the concept 'millions of years', nor the fact that the phrase betrays the presuppositions of geological orthodoxy, rather than established fact. However, it is surely natural to suppose that the children are just as likely to remember the words of the phrases as they are the piece of music. What will the child have learned at the end of this lesson? The six year old may have learned about musical pitch and rhythm. It is much more likely that what they will have learned is that 'fossils are millions of years old'. The teaching of contentious views as fact used to be known as indoctrination. Our children are being indoctrinated in their schools.

Understandable error

It is not my contention that these examples are necessarily deliberate attempts to deceive. Although educationalists are striving for greater scientific literacy among teachers in general, it is still the case that a non-science subject specialist cannot be expected to be up to date with all aspects of science. Where should such experts look for their scientific views? It would be proper for them to expect to be able to trust the science education experts to give them valid information. The music teacher who wrote the example above has not, in my opinion, sought to deceive or indoctrinate, despite my use of the word. Indeed, her choice of example is a laudable attempt to enable an opportunity for cross-curricular teaching. Her example would undoubtedly be approved by educational experts in fields such as biology or geology. The blame for such errors must still be laid at the door of science education.

Notes

1 Science in the National Curriculum in Wales, ACCAC: 2000, p. 31.

2 Ibid. p. 38.

3 Science: The National Curriculum for England, QCA: 1999, p. 49.

4 Mathematics: The National Curriculum for England, QCA: 1999.

5 *Where did the universe come from?*,
   http://www.standards.dfes.gov.uk/pdf/secondaryschemes/rel9b.pdf

6 Ibid.

7 Ibid.

8 Ibid.

9 **R. Grigg,** 'Did Moses Really Write Genesis', *Creation* **20**(4): 43–46.

10 Religious, Moral and Philosophical Studies Higher (Scottish Qualifications Authority: 2005), p. 55.

11 Ibid. p. 56.

12 Music: National Curriculum for England, section Mu 4b, http://www.nc.uk.net/nc/contents/Mu-1--POS.html

13 **H. MacGregor,** *Music Express: Year 2* (London: A & C Black, 2002), pp. 31–32.

Towards a biblical approach

It would not be correct to title this final section 'Conclusions', because the matter cannot be concluded. Science education is developing, and some of these developments are outside the control of concerned Christians, whether teachers, parents, pastors or students. Rather, it will be necessary to issue a number of 'points to ponder' on which Christians will need to dwell in order to make informed decisions on education.

This book has contained a number of concerns about the current direction of science education. It is possible that some of these concerns were not known previously by many Christian parents, for example. These parents may feel the need to respond to the issues raised. These responses will be various, ranging from homeschooling their children, using Christian schools, or taking a more pro-active and prayerful role in the state comprehensives. Our approaches will be influenced in large measure by our circumstances and by the relative importance we place on the summaries given in this chapter.

The true nature of science

We have seen that science and spirituality cannot legitimately be separated. Our studies have taken us through the works of historical figures, dealing with their own understandings of the natural world, and we have seen how their understanding of the spiritual has influenced their scientific understanding.

We have observed how the writers of the National Curriculum in science have sought to reflect this issue in their insistence on science being taught within a context and that pupils should have an appreciation of the contexts within which the science is practised.

We have seen the historic reasons for the attempts to separate what is spiritual from what is natural. This bipartite view of the cosmos has been criticised but its importance to current thinking on science has been recognised. The orthodoxy of such an approach has led to the general public's assumption that science must always stand on its own without reference to ideas of God or the supernatural. Despite the inclusion of

National Curriculum comments on the contexts of science, it is recognised that science education in state schools in the UK is largely influenced by this 'no God' approach, to the extent that any reference to God in the teaching of any part of the knowledge or understanding contents of science is seen as anathema.

Parents usually want to help their children. Science (in common with maths) is a subject where many parents feel unable to offer help and support. So much has changed over the last thirty years about our knowledge of science and particularly how it is taught. Yet science is a core subject in the National Curriculum, and compulsory in England and Wales to the age of sixteen. Hopefully, this work will go some way towards helping Christian parents to understand a little more about what is going on in the science education scene, and will enable them to make more informed decisions about their children's' futures.

Bringing back the Bible

It has also been shown that the Bible has a great deal to say on the subject of education in general and therefore by inference of science education in particular. It has been noted that education is first and foremost the duty of the parent rather than the state. The studies have been as pragmatic as possible, implying that parents may delegate this educational responsibility to those whom they trust, but that this delegation in no wise removes their responsibility for the education of their children.

Martin Luther's famous comment is pertinent at this point.

I would advise no one to send his child where the Holy Scriptures are not supreme. Every institution that does not unceasingly pursue the study of God's word becomes corrupt.[1]

Luther's concern for children is one that should be echoed by present generations of Christian parents. How those parents work out their reactions to these issues is for them to decide prayerfully before God. It is the eternal destiny of our children which is at stake, so Luther exhorts us to consider these matters very seriously. He goes on to talk about the educational institutions of his day, and how damaging they were to young people. One wonders what he would have said about our universities.

I greatly fear that the universities, unless they teach the Holy Scriptures diligently and impress them on the young students, are wide gates to hell.[2]

It might seem a little melodramatic to think of our state schools as 'wide gates to hell', but that is what they are if they are leading our young people away from knowledge of Jesus Christ and the truth of his word.

Classroom concerns

Our studies have seen that, despite protestations of the religious neutrality of science, modern scientific ideas are actually pregnant with religious opinion—even if that opinion is that religion is wrong. The mystical nature of much that is stated in modern physics has been noted.

Discussions of classroom practice have led to some practical propositions on how to respond to the spiritual contexts of science. Concern has then been expressed that certain classroom practice in fully secularising science teaching has led to a negation of scientific methodology.

It is the opinion of this author that Christian parents need to return to the principle that they are the ones who have the main responsibility to educate their children. It is the responsibility of parents to see that their children are educated in accordance with biblical principles. Some parents may recognise a need to be more fully involved in the curriculum decisions of their state schools. Some parents will want to take more radical steps by home-schooling their children, or supporting independent Christian schools.

My own views have altered on the subject over the years. I once had a letter published in a Christian newspaper opposing Christian education. In recent years, my change of opinion has been quoted in print by Sylvia Baker, former headteacher of Trinity School, Stalybridge, in a letter I wrote to her.

I thought it was time I wrote to you because in the past we used to differ over the subject of Christian education. I have now come to the view that my previous opposition to independent Christian education was wrong …

I now see a society ever more out of touch with God. I see an education system ever more out of touch with God. I see an education system ever more geared to training young people away from Christian values. I now believe that a school such as yours, open to the public but working with Christian staff in a Christian ethos is a valuable and powerful witness to the nation.[3]

This may not be the answer that every Christian parent wants to accept, but I strongly urge all Christian parents to consider their positions with regard to the education of their children, particularly in the light of some of the issues expressed in this book.

Notes

1 **Martin Luther,** *To the Christian Nobility of the German Nation Concerning the Reform of the Christian Estate, 1520,* trans. **Charles M. Jacobs,** rev. **James Atkinson,** *The Christian in Society,* I (*Luther's Works,* ed. James Atkinson, vol. 44), p. 207 (1966).

2 Ibid.

3 **Paul Taylor,** personal letter to Sylvia Baker, quoted in **S. Baker** and **D. Freeman,** *The Love of God in the Classroom* (Fearn, Tain: Christian Focus Publications, 2005), p. 41.

Genesis for today
The relevance of the creation/
evolution debate to today's society

ANDY MCINTOSH

240PP ILLUSTRATED PAPERBACK

ISBN 978-1-84625-051-4

Professor McIntosh is a scientist who sees no contradiction between science and the events of creation in the book of Genesis. He believes that all Christian doctrine, directly or indirectly, has its basis in the literal events of the first eleven chapters of the Bible, and that these foundations of the faith are being undermined in the church by the fallible theories of evolution.

'For those who have eyes to see, here is ample proof that God's revealed truth is as trustworthy as ever—and infinitely more certain than every human speculation.'
—JOHN MACARTHUR

EDGAR POWELL

280PP, PAPERBACK

ISBN 978 0 902548 93 0

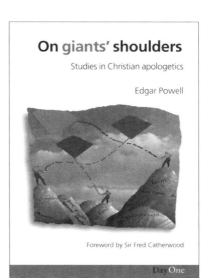

On giants' shoulders

Studies in Christian apologetics

Edgar Powell

Foreword by Sir Fred Catherwood

DayOne

If you want facts with which to answer evolutionists, this book will help. It takes conviction and courage to stand up for the gospel and this book readily responds, with thought-provoking answers, to the propaganda from evolutionists.

Edgar Powell, BSc, MSc, PGCE, is a curriculum director in computing in a further education college. He teaches computing, information technology and geology, having over thirty years' teaching experience. He has contributed articles to *Creation Research Quarterly*, *Evangelicals Now*, *Evangelical Times*, *Grace Magazine* and *Monthly Record*. He and his wife have two daughters.

'A splendid overview of contemporary apologetic challenges.'
—*CHRISTIANITY TODAY*

'… an outstanding achievement … food for thought on every page.'
—*PROFESSOR WILLIAM EDGAR, WESTMINSTER THEOLOGICAL SEMINARY, PHILADELPHIA*

Hallmarks of design:
Evidence of design in the natural world

STUART BURGESS

256PP, ILLUSTRATED PAPERBACK

ISBN 978 1 903087 31 2

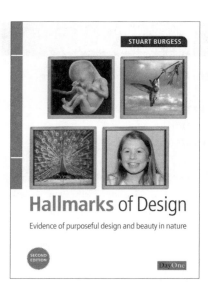

The Design Argument contends that design in nature reveals a Designer. *Hallmarks of Design* presents this in the light of the latest discoveries about the complexity and beauty of the natural world. Features of the book include:

- Six clear hallmarks of design;
- Over thirty diagrams;
- Description of how the earth is designed for mankind;
- Description of the Creator's attributes

Dr Stuart Burgess is Head of Department of Mechanical Engineering at the University of Bristol. His research areas include the study of design in nature. He previously worked in industry, designing rocket and satellite systems for the European Space Agency. He is winner of the Worshipful Company of Turners Gold Medal for the design of the solar array deployment system on the £1·4 billion ENVISAT earth observation satellite.

'Compelling presentation of the evidence of design in the natural world.'
—*BANNER OF TRUTH MAGAZINE*

He made the stars also:
What the Bible says about the stars

STUART BURGESS

192PP, ILLUSTRATED PAPERBACK

ISBN 978 1 903087 13 8

He made the
stars also

The origin and purpose of the stars

Stuart Burgess

DayOne

This book teaches clearly and biblically the purpose of the stars and the question of extra-terrestrial life. Dr Burgess explains how the earth has a unique purpose in supporting life and how the stars have a singular purpose in shining light on it. He explains why the universe contains such natural beauty and how the stars reveal God's character.

Dr Stuart Burgess is Head of Department of Mechanical Engineering at the University of Bristol. His research areas include the study of design in nature. He previously worked in industry, designing rocket and satellite systems for the European Space Agency. He is winner of the Worshipful Company of Turners Gold Medal for the design of the solar array deployment system on the £1·4 billion ENVISAT earth observation satellite.

'Dr Burgess has a very clear style and his book brims with interesting material. It will be greatly appreciated.'
—DR PETER MASTERS, METROPOLITAN TABERNACLE

The origin of man:
The image of God or the image of an ape?

STUART BURGESS

192PP, ILLUSTRATED PAPERBACK

ISBN 978 1 903087 73 2

Have humans descended from apes or were they specially created? Do humans have unique characteristics and abilities that set them apart from all the animals? The answers to these crucial questions determine whether man is just an animal or a special spiritual being. There is overwhelming evidence that man has a Creator. This book contains many diagrams and includes:

- Explanation of similarities between humans and apes;
- Unique characteristics and abilities of humans;
- Unique beauty of humans;
- Archaeological and fossil evidence;
- The importance and relevance of the origins debate.

Dr Stuart Burgess is Head of Department of Mechanical Engineering at the University of Bristol. His research areas include the study of design in nature. He previously worked in industry, designing rocket and satellite systems for the European Space Agency. He is winner of the Worshipful Company of Turners Gold Medal for the design of the solar array deployment system on the £1·4 billion ENVISAT earth observation satellite.

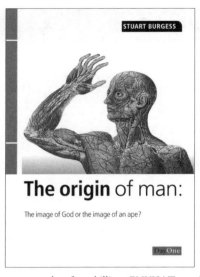

STUART BURGESS

The origin of man:

The image of God or the image of an ape?

Day One

Life's story—The one that hasn't been told

MARK HAVILLE

64PP, PAPERBACK, POCKET BOOK SIZE,
ILLUSTRATED IN COLOUR THROUGHOUT

ISBN 978 903087 71 8

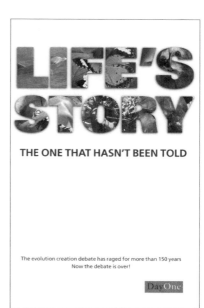

THE ONE THAT HASN'T BEEN TOLD

The evolution creation debate has raged for more than 150 years
Now the debate is over!

DayOne

Written for anyone who is interested in the creation/evolution debate, but doesn't know where to start, this highly illustrated guide is the perfect introduction to the subject. Exploring the arguments, author Mark Haville thoughtfully analyses the flaws in the theory of natural selection. Beautifully illustrated in full colour throughout.

Mark Haville is a biblical creationist with a wide-ranging ministry.

'The photography is breathtaking, the science is crystal clear and the application is thoroughly biblical. *Life's Story* is surely contender for 'Best in its class'.'
—*DR JOHN BLANCHARD, REVIEWING THE DVD ON WHICH THE BOOK IS BASED*

The design and origin of birds

PHILIP SNOW

256PP PAPERBACK, ILLUSTRATED THROUGHOUT

ISBN 978 1 84625 002 6

Birds are amongst the world's most beautiful and beloved parts of creation, so it is not surprising that they have been so widely studied. This book closely examines their wonderful aerial lifestyle and unique, warm-blooded design—often so different from the cold-blooded dinosaurs that they are claimed to have accidentally 'evolved' from This fascinating and beautifully produced book brings to light important facts from the world of science and is illustrated throughout by the author.

Philip Snow is a wildlife and landscape painter, illustrator and writer. His work appears in many publications and galleries, and he has illustrated, or contributed work to, over sixty books, and many magazines, prints, cards, calendars, reserve guides and decorated maps etc.

'Birds have played an important part in human history and have always been respected and loved for hreir beauty and amazing flying skills. Philip Snow has produced a unique book which expertly describes and illustrates the design, life and beauty of birds.'
—*STUART BURGESS, PROFESSOR OF DESIGN AND NATURE, UNIVERSITY OF BRISTOL*

An interview with C H Spurgeon
—C H Spurgeon on creation and evolution

DAVID HARDING

128PP PAPERBACK

ISBN 978 1 84625 021 7

C H Spurgeon, who is known to be theologically robust about the verbal inspiration, infallibility, perspicuity and preservation of the text of the Bible, made many forthright statements about Darwinism and his sermons and writings are liberally sprinkled with references to the subject. In this 'virtual' interview, David Harding takes us through his general thoughts on the matter, on science and the Bible, and then his more specific attitudes to science. There is advice to young people and then comments for preachers. What of those who disagree? He had a few words for them too The appendix explores Spurgeon's attitude to his own fallibility and is relevant in view of his opinions and judgements about when the world was made.

David Harding is pastor of the Milnrow Evangelical Church, Lancashire, England, where he has ministered for the last thirteen years. His background was in local government work and he has also been an elder at Garforth Evangelical Church, and an evangelist and elder at Flitwick Baptist Church. He and his wife, Colette, have two adult sons, Matthew and Joel.

'A masterpiece of writing'

—*ANDY C. MCINTOSH DSC, FIMA, C.MATH, FEI, C.ENG, FINSTP, MIGEM, FRAES, PROFESSOR OF THERMODYNAMICS AND COMBUSTION THEORY, UNIVERSITY OF LEEDS*

'… A lucid, forceful, definitive, biblical answer to the theory of evolution in Spurgeon's own words. … invaluable for both its historic significance and its timeless insight. I'm delighted to see this book in print.'

—*PHIL JOHNSON, GRACE TO YOU, USA*